D0938965

THE CENTRE FOR ENVIRONMENTAL STUDIES SERIES
General Editor: Christopher Forster

LEAVING LONDON

This book is one of a series edited at the Centre for Environmental Studies and published on its behalf by Heinemann Educational Books Ltd. The series will present work in the fields of planning, and urban and regional studies. The Centre is an independent research foundation charged with the furtherance and dissemination of research in these fields. Further information about this series and the Centre's work can be obtained from the General Editor.

Leaving London

Planned Mobility and the Inner City

NICHOLAS DEAKIN
CLARE UNGERSON

 Heinemann : London

Heinemann Educational Books Ltd

London Edinburgh Melbourne Auckland Toronto
Hong Kong Singapore Kuala Lumpur
Ibadan Nairobi Johannesburg
Lusaka New Delhi
Kingston

ISBN 0 435 85930 7

Published by Heinemann Educational Books Ltd
48 Charles Street, London W1X 8AH

Filmset in Great Britain by
Northumberland Press Ltd, Gateshead, Tyne and Wear
and printed by
Richard Clay (The Chaucer Press), Ltd,
Bungay, Suffolk

Contents

Preface

The germ of this study lay in a single observation. One of the present writers was then working on a programme of race relations studies; one of the separate investigations commissioned as part of the programme was a study of housing policies [1]. In the course of discussing the progress of the work, the researcher observed that there was one sector of the housing market that had so far not been penetrated by coloured immigrants: the New Towns. The reason seemed at first sight rather difficult to understand. Having taken the decision to migrate several thousand miles into what was usually, for the newcomers, an entirely strange environment, it hardly seemed logical that they should baulk at a further short move—particularly one which could reward them with greatly improved housing conditions and amenities. Furthermore, the immigrant population—in particular the Asian migrants—was already widely distributed through a whole range of towns of various sizes. The crucial factor in determining this distribution, as Dr Ceri Peach had shown some time before [2], was the availability of employment; and by the late fifties, when the migration was reaching what proved to be its peak, the New Towns were already over their early teething problems and beginning to attract employment on a considerable scale.

There was no particular originality in this observation; in fact, several other interested observers had commented on the same point at about the same time [3]. But the questions that it raised remained unanswered; furthermore, it linked up with a topic that had also begun to attract attention—the question of the feasibility of promoting the planned dispersal of ethnic minorities. One of us had been asked to give evidence to the Sub-committee of the Central Housing Advisory Committee which was then investigating access to Council housing, under the chairmanship of Professor Barry Cullingworth [4]. The Committee struggled manfully with the issue of dispersal, and the problems that it posed for public authorities. After quoting at some length from the evidence we had submitted, the Committee concluded that no hard and fast guidelines could yet be laid down; pending their appearance, the guiding principle should be that dispersal must be a matter of individual choice. The Committee supplemented this conclusion with the traditional recommendation that further research should be undertaken.

The resulting opportunity had obvious attractions. Movement to New Towns provided a particularly good test case for a study, it seemed to us, because it posed the option of voluntary dispersal in a particularly appealing form. In John Barr's phrase, the New Towns could serve as 'anti-ghettoes'—the opposite side of the coin from the congested inner urban areas in which immigrants were becoming concentrated. That a push factor existed, in terms of the poor conditions in those areas and the discrimination often encountered there, seemed clear [5]; the obvious question to ask was whether the planned environment of the New Towns could exert an equivalent pull. The existence of a complex set of administrative procedures governing entry into this new environment—the complexities of which we only dimly understood at this stage—offered an opportunity of establishing how far discrimination, either intentional or as an unintended consequence of mechanisms established for other purposes, was a relevant factor in the situation.

However, when we made our first tentative approaches about the possibility of obtaining funds for the study of the movement of blacks to New Towns, several objections were raised, both by those whose advice we sought and by the Committee of the Social Science Research Council to which we first submitted the proposal. In essence, the argument was that immigrants from the New Commonwealth made up a group with special characteristics. Their failure to establish themselves in New Towns might be the result of those special factors, and have no relevance to the broader questions of recruitment of population from London. On the other hand, a comparative study, in which the problems experienced by immigrants were placed alongside those of other groups disadvantaged in a number of different ways, would enable us to assess how far difficulties flowed from factors peculiar to the race (or, more politely, ethnic origin) of potential migrants, and how far they were the product of general disadvantages, like poverty, or lack of access to relevant information. The study would have more interest, in short, if it were placed 'in a broader context'—a phrase we were to come to know well.

Such a study would have the additional virtue of being more closely related to previous thinking about the objectives of New Towns policy. The original 'Mark 1' New Towns had been intended as balanced communities, both economically and socially; this was an objective that went back to Ebenezer Howard's original formulation of a 'Social City', which catered for all sections of the population. The extent to which this goal had been achieved by the first wave of London New Towns was, of course, arguable; but the second wave of 'Mark 2 New Towns' which had begun to get under way by the middle sixties was expressly intended to make good this deficiency. In Milton Keynes, perhaps the best publicized of them all, the Corporation had proclaimed in their 'Interim Report' that 'it is the Corporation's policy to aim at social balance in the population of the new city. This means that, so far as possible, the city must attract all sorts of people, where earlier New Towns have tended to attract mainly people within certain ranges of age, population and income' [6]. Our preliminary discussions with the Corporation indicated that they specifically intended to try to ensure that coloured immigrants would be among the range of people for whom Milton Keynes would cater.

The argument therefore seemed convincing; and we accordingly revised our initial approach, and broadened the scope of the study to cover 'disadvantaged groups' generally. Our proposal in its final form was therefore for a study that would assess the scope for movement by these minorities to New (and Expanding) Towns in London and the South-East, and the experience of some of those who had succeeded in making the move. After some delay, the application was approved by the Social Science Research Council, and we began work in January 1971.

We took as the starting point of our study eight questions which we had formulated about the dispersal of disadvantaged minorities from London. First, what evidence was there to suggest that the opportunity for dispersal existed? Second, if opportunities proved not to exist in practice, what were the constraints preventing them from being available to these groups? Third, if they were available, even on a limited scale, to what extent were individuals from the groups in question aware of them? Fourth, if—or when—they did become aware of them, what decided such individuals to attempt to move to a New or Expanded Town? Fifth, what were the obstacles that impeded them once they had taken such a decision; and sixth, at what stages in the process of planned migration did these obstacles assume particular importance for these groups? Seventh, what reasons impelled those who abandoned the attempt to do so (both subjective reasons—attitudes towards the administrative machinery or New Towns—and objective ones—i.e. discrimination on the grounds of race) and, eighth, what was the reaction of those who eventually succeeded in obtaining access to the New (or Expanding) Towns? To what extent did they experience practical or psychological problems of adjustment?

Having decided to place the main emphasis on the problems of the Inner City, it followed that the logical sequence in which to follow through these questions was in their geographical order, from the Inner City outwards. Thus one of the most important decisions became the choice of the deprived area for study. In choosing it we had three criteria in mind; first, the extent of deprivation; second, the representation in the neighbourhood of the deprived groups in which we had expressed particular interest—unskilled workers, those living in housing stress and the ethnic minorities; and, third, evidence that the borough concerned had in the past exported a substantial population to New or Expanding Towns. The area finally selected for study, the Highbury and Parkway Wards of Islington, satisfied all these three criteria; within the project team, Garry McDonald was responsible for the study.

The second stage in the study was concerned with alternative ways in which the migration can be undertaken, and the circumstances in which the opportunity to undertake it arises. The study of the Industrial Selection Scheme[1] (ISS) explored the characteristics of the groups that move through the official machinery—in this case, through a detailed re-analysis of data from the scheme made available to us by the GLC. Since one main way of moving to a New Town is to work for a firm that makes the

---

[1] After this study was completed, the name of the Scheme was changed; it is now known as the New and Expanding Towns Scheme (NETS). In the present text it will be referred to by the name it bore at the time when the research was undertaken, except where the context requires otherwise.

decision to move to a New or Expanding Town, a study of two firms that were about to move provided us with an opportunity to assess the factors that individuals presented with the concrete opportunity to move take into account when they make the decision whether to go or not. The first of these two studies was undertaken by Charles Thomson, the second by Ukwu Ejionye.

In addition to the analysis of those moving through the ISS, and the migrant firms study, an investigation was undertaken of a group of migrants who had moved from Islington—the intention being to throw further light on the question of choice, and the grounds on which the decision to move was taken. This study connects with a second, and less formal, investigation of the outcome of migration for a group of employees of one of the migrant firms. Both these studies were undertaken by Clare Ungerson.

The third study of individuals who had made the move to the new environment was a study of one particular potentially disadvantaged group in one New Town—the Asians in Crawley. The researcher responsible for this stage of the study was Audrey Maxwell.

The report that follows is not the report of these original studies. A report incorporating all of them was presented to the Social Science Research Council in June 1973 and some of the results of the individual studies and a summary of the main results of the whole project have been published elsewhere [7], [8], [9]. What follows is an attempt to distil some of the more important (or surprising) results into a coherent whole; it draws mainly on the work done in the Islington housing stress area and the survey of people who had recently moved from the London Borough of Islington to a New or Expanding Town. Nevertheless, where data from the other surveys are relevant and illuminating we have included them. As it turns out, the focus of the study is now more on the 'Inner City' and its residents and their opportunities to live elsewhere, than on New Towns and their potential to absorb current residents of the Inner City. This bias (if that is the right term) arises partly from the balance of the material available to us; but it is also the result of the opportunity that we have had, since the completion of the original report, to mull over the findings and try to assess their significance for some of the broader debates that have been taking place about the Inner City.

We plead guilty to having taken our time over this further consideration of the evidence: we must hope that the use that we have been able to make of it, in terms both of elucidating the reasons for recent social changes in the city and of exploring the issues arising from those changes, will help to compensate for the delay.

July 1977   Nicholas Deakin *and* Clare Ungerson

References

1. BURNEY, E., *Housing on Trial* (Oxford University Press, for Institute of Race Relations, 1967).

2. PEACH, C., *West Indian Migration to Britain* (OUP for Institute of Race Relations, 1968).

3. JOHN BARR, 'New towns as anti-ghettoes?', *New Society*, 1 April 1965, pp. 5–6.

4. Ministry of Housing and Local Government, *Council Housing: Purposes, Procedures and Priorities* (The 'Cullingworth Report') (HMSO, 1969).

5. BURNEY, *Housing on Trial* (op. cit.).

6. LLEWELYN-DAVIES, WEEKS, FORESTIER-WALKER and BOR, *Milton Keynes Plan: Interim report to the Milton Keynes Development Corporation* (1968). See pp. 30 ff., 'Social development'.

7. DEAKIN, N. and UNGERSON, C., 'The Non-Movers?', *Town and Country Planning*, January 1974.

8. CHARLES THOMSON, *The Industrial Selection Scheme—a study of conflicting objectives in urban and regional planning* (Centre for Environmental Studies WP81, 1973).

9. McDONALD, G., 'Metropolitan Housing Policy and the Stress Areas', *Urban Studies*, **11**, 34, 1974.

Acknowledgments

It remains to thank all those who have helped us with the project. The original report was a collective exercise by the research team. We are therefore principally indebted to Ukwu Ejionye, Garry McDonald, Audrey Maxwell, and Charles Thomson who carried out the separate studies described above. Where appropriate, we have indicated in the text where we are drawing directly on material for which they were wholly or partly responsible, within the original project. There were two other indispensable members of the team—the Project Secretary, Rosemary Lewin, and Nanneke Redclift. Next, we would like to acknowledge the help of Brian Cohen, who first formulated the original proposal to do work in this field. At the Centre for Environmental Studies, apart from the then Director, Professor David Donnison, who was most helpful at all stages of the project we would like to thank Peter Marris, David Eversley, Mike Harloe, Christine Adnitt, Gill Snowball, Neil Piercy and Doris Cook. Adrian Barritt helped with the footnotes and bibliography.

Members of the Urban Studies seminar at the University of Kent, particularly Murray Stewart, Ray Pahl ,and Nanneke Redclift were of great help to Clare Ungerson.

Others who have assisted in the course of the project are Peter Willmott, Anne Swingler, Lee Shostak, Bernard Crofton, Hardev Singh, Peter Sonley, L. J. Furneaux, D. R. Moon, K. Gambier; members of the London Dispersal Liaison Group, officers of the GLC Industrial Centre; London Borough of Islington Planning and Housing Departments; SHAC, the GLC Housing Department—in particular R. D. Kerswell, R. W. Stephens, P. Heinecke, and staff of the New and Expanding Towns section; the London Boroughs Association; the Department of Environment New Towns Directorate—in particular H. Griffiths and W. P. Roderick; and the Department of Employment London and South East Regional Office—in particular D. C. Wycherley. Finally, in addition to the help that several of them gave in other ways, David Donnison, David Eversley, Arthur Fleiss, Murray Stewart, Chris Pickvance, Graham Lomas and Peter Willmott read and commented on drafts of this book. Margaret Orchard organized the production of the final typescript and Pauline Nicholson typed it; we are grateful to them, too.

We would also like to thank Ellen Johnson and Jean Morton-Williams of Social and Community Planning Research and Graham Read and John Samuels of the British Market Research Bureau. Most of all, our thanks are due to the thousand men and women who gave time to the interviewers who landed on their doorsteps and, through what they told them, gave us the basis for much of this report.

We are grateful to all of these people for their help; we—and not they—are responsible for mistakes and omissions. Finally, it should be recorded that since February 1972, Nicholas Deakin has been a member of the staff of the Greater London Council: the Council is not, however, responsible in any way for the views expressed in this Report.

N.D. *and* C.U.

Chapter One

Deciding to Leave the City

The Concept of Choice

The preface to this volume described briefly the five studies that
contributed to the discussion here, and indicated that there were
eight questions that lay behind the work the project team did
when considering the movement of disadvantaged minorities to
New Towns. These questions covered the opportunities that
existed for moving; the reason why such opportunities were or
were not available to particular individuals or groups; the extent
to which people were aware of them; the process of movement;
the obstacles that impeded it; the importance that these obstacles
assumed, and, for the unsuccessful, the reasons for abandoning
the attempt to move; for the successful, their reaction on finally
attaining their destination.

The key concept in this discussion was the question of choice.
Did our respondents have real choice to stay where they were
or move to a New or Expanding Town; if they had that choice,
how did they exercise it; if not, how would they have exercised
it if it had been given to them; who or what constrained those
choices? But 'choice' itself proved to be an extremely elusive
concept—how was 'real choice' to be defined? Clearly, we could
not assume that because people behaved in a particular way
or because they said they wanted to behave in a particular way,
their object of apparent choice was not itself subject to severe
constraints. To some other researchers working on similar
problems the whole approach through choice seems futile. They
argue that: 'to conduct research into choice, voluntariness or
preference in so constrained and competitive a market situation
is merely the indulgence of an ideology which promises what

it cannot deliver' [1]. But even in a constrained situation, choices are still being made—indeed, they may be of particular importance just because opportunities are limited. So, although the concept of choice itself is a slippery one and difficult to put into operation in terms of writing questionnaires for social surveys, we were still attracted to the idea of observing actual behaviour and drawing some tentative inferences about choice, and, more particularly, constraints on choice from these observations. For example, if we could show that particular people—such as the families of young, white, skilled, male manual workers— appeared to move more frequently to New and Expanding Towns than other people with different observable characteristics, then we could make one of two inferences about choice— or both. The first would be that these people, with such characteristics, were more likely to wish to move than others; the second would be that these people were less constrained in their choices since the selection process for migrants assessed their characteristics favourably.

The obvious difficulty with these two inferences was that they could be both contradictory and complementary. They could be contradictory in the sense that one inference might be the exhaustive explanation of behaviour—for example, very high motivation on the part of potential migrants might actually be enough to overcome the measurable constraints, or, alternatively, lack of constraints might be a positive factor in pushing even reluctant migrants to New or Expanding Towns. They could be complementary in the sense that potential migrants might be encouraged by the relative lack of constraints in their particular case. Moreover, the difficulty in making either of these inferences about choice from behaviour was compounded by the fact that there were at least two different routes to New and Expanding Towns: one, through the Industrial Selection Scheme, where the potential migrant had to be motivated enough to register his or her name on a list of willing movers; the other, through working for a firm that made the decision to move. In the first situation the constraints might be formidable, in the latter, they might hardly exist, and either situation might apply to people of identical observable characteristics. Thus, both within each of the surveys carried out for this research and between them, it would prove to be extremely difficult to make generalizations about how Inner London residents had 'chosen' in the past or might 'choose' in the future. Nor was it really possible to predict whether a constraint relaxed in one institution would mean that particular defined groups of people would move to a New or Expanding Town. The links between motivation and opportunity proved difficult to unravel; like cogs in a motor they moved in conjunction, interdependently, and their end result was visible and measurable. But their independent power remained unknown. Nevertheless, we could still speculate about what the elements of such choices or constraints might be, even though we might not be able to weigh the relative significance of these elements.

In attempting to disentangle these complexities, we drew on the sociological and anthropological traditions, with varying commitment to considerations of policy. But, when writing the questionnaires for the social surveys that made up a crucial part of the study, we found ourselves employing cruder questions, drawn unsystematically from a multitude of traditions and theories—many of which contradicted or were inconsistent with each other. For example, were those people who had lived longer in a particular area the most reluctant to move? (This point will be developed much more fully later.) Were people who were likely to lose their jobs unless they moved keener to go? Were those in decent local authority housing in the Inner City happy to stay where they were? In selecting these questions we were subscribing to the views that among other factors, local 'roots', job security, decent housing, were all push and pull elements in the migration process.

At the same time, we were concerned with another set of questions. Similar studies of residents of Inner City areas, migrants to suburbs or New Towns, and moving firms raised the issue: how different from or how like the respondents in these studies are our own samples? What do these similarities or differences indicate about the kinds of people who have in the past moved to New Towns or may move in the future—given a foreseeable world with all other things equal? In this sense, we were asking questions that used disciplinary *traditions* rather than theory as their bench-marks. We were repeating well-tried questions on yet another group of Inner City residents or New Town dwellers to discover whether they were poorer, younger, blacker, less skilled, more skilled, less 'friendly' or more 'friendly' than previous studies had found. Once we found differences between our samples and others we would have to ask the question 'why?'

This process could lead forward in three ways. First, we could speculate that our samples were atypical—that there were special features external to the respondents that explained the differences we had discovered between our respondents and others. For example, the particular location of our respondents might be the reason that made them behave or think in ways different from samples from other areas. Second, the samples might be typical but differences between them explained by time—that is, a context of general social change over time explained why previous studies and our own differed. Third, we could use our empirical data to extend the theories that had been used in the past to explain previous empirical data, or to pinpoint apparent gaps or contradictions within that theory.

In sum, then, we did not set out to test one particular (sociological) theory. Rather, by approaching the issues through the question of choice we tried to discern the elements that might determine and constrain those choices. Our study is based on the tradition of British urban sociology, although the approach that we have adopted has been a complex, occasionally confused, and probably circular one. For example, the work of the Institute of Community Studies [2] influenced us heavily, and we emphasized in all our surveys the hypothesis that close links with relatives within a 'small' Inner City area might prevent people from moving since the costs in terms of social contacts and mutual aid might be perceived to be too great. Similarly, drawing on studies of the development of suburbs, we were curious how far movers were more 'aspirant' than non-movers.

The discussion that follows attempts two things. First, by looking at the writing that can be called 'British urban sociology' and 'urban history' we hope to draw out some of the points made in the past that appear most salient to the research results reported in the rest of this volume. Second, the discussion should provide a framework which we can use to explore and analyse the results of the research project in a coherent way. But throughout it must be remembered that this framework is part of a circular process: the clue for it lay partly in the initial tabulations that emerged after the five studies were completed, and out of the framework itself should come clues to the 'reality' behind the tabulations.

Some Key Perspectives

There are four strands which have run through post-war British urban sociology which have particular relevance to the movement of 'disadvantaged minorities' to New and Expanding Towns. These have been the concept of 'community' and its application to inner areas of cities, and the concept of a heterogeneous working class with divisions into 'rough' and 'respectable'. Another concept that is directly relevant is of the heterogeneous suburb where 'respectable' people who share common values particularly about child-rearing will attempt to congregate; fourthly, and much more recently, there is the concept of 'urban managerialism'. But the first two concepts, when taken together, present an important difficulty: the concept of community appears to assume a homogeneous working class, whereas the rough/respectable dichotomy implies the opposite. Thus any attempt to test the pull of 'community' as a factor preventing members of that community from moving away must be counterbalanced by the hypothesis that there are many apparent members of that community who would like to reject it, given the opportunity, on the grounds that it is not 'respectable' enough for them. So there is considerable tension —if not contradiction—between these two concepts in British urban sociology, which is made more complex by the introduction of the notion of location. Given that 'community' has within it a sense of location, and that it is often suggested that the 'respectable' will attempt to move to the suburbs, which *are* a location, then the tension between attachment to community and the values pertaining to particular social status will inevitably colour the migration process.

The 'community'

As Bell and Newby [3] point out, the concept of community and its study are really will-o'-the-wisps—if attractive ones. Having tried to discover elements basic either to the concept or to its numerous studies they confess:

> Rather as intelligence is what intelligence tests measure perhaps we can, for the time being at any rate, merely treat community as what community studies analyse [4].

Yet the concept of community, ill-defined (or undefinable) as it is, has played a central part in the discussion of post-war British urban sociology. Many studies, particularly in the middle fifties made the 'community' the central core of their investigation [5]. The best-known of these studies came from the Institute of Community Studies which was founded in 1954 expressly to study the community and problems of Bethnal Green. In *Family and Kinship in East London* [6], Michael Young and Peter Willmott set out to assess the effect of local authority housing dispersal policies on family life in Bethnal Green. Among their findings they found what they claimed to be a 'sense of community'.

> There is a sense of community, that is a feeling of solidarity between people who occupy the common territory, which springs from the fact that people and their families have lived there a long time [7].

But although Young and Willmott argued that Bethnal Green residents enjoyed this 'network of local attachment' and wished to remain amongst their friends and relatives, the authors did imply that there were some disadvantages accruing to this way of life: 'If you know other people's business, they know yours. Feuds may be all the more bitter for being contained in such small space.'

However, in the following sentence they add:

> But there are advantages too. For many people, familiarity breeds content. Bethnal Greeners are not lonely people: whenever they go for a walk in the street, for a drink in the pub or for a row on the lake in Victoria Park, they know the faces in the crowd [8].

Thus within Young and Willmott's first work there was a tension between those who liked the 'village' of Bethnal Green and those who had reason not to, but this was a tension the authors chose to underplay. Indeed they concluded that it was the very 'sense of community' which acted as a positive disincentive to move.

> The view that we have formed and tested more or less daily for three years is that very few people wish to leave the East End. They are attached to Mum and Dad, to the markets, to the pubs and settlements, to Club Row and the London Hospital [9].

Thus there arose the notion of the 'Village in the City'—a concept not confined to British urban sociology but fully developed in the American literature as well [10]. In both cases, it is arguable that those who claimed to have discovered such a 'village' in whatever urban context they were studying liked it, and that is why they chose to emphasize it. They liked the notion that despite rapid industrialization, urbanization, concomitant and contextual rapid social change, and the development of contractual impersonal relationships rather than intimate personal relationships, there still remained areas where relationships were intimate, orderly and loyal. It seems that to many commentators the *village* in the City is the saving grace of otherwise graceless cities. Indeed, it is suggested that part of the dialectic of the City is to throw up homogeneous, intimate communities as self-defence against the City's very anonymity. Thus Nicholas Taylor in his book on the Edwardian and Victorian suburbs of London claims that:

> within the major cities there is a psychological understandable inclination for the individual to withdraw from the broad built-up mass into a group of half-a-dozen streets with a corner shop and a pub [11].

There is no doubt that the arguments embodied in the Institute of Community Studies' early work, particularly those about the strength of community ties within an urban context, have had an enormous influence on the planning profession, urban sociology, and the lay public. Young and Willmott themselves concluded *Family and Kinship in East London* with the suggestion that efforts should be made by planners and housing managers to maintain the community despite urban renewal either by dispersing residents as a unity or rehousing Bethnal Greeners in Bethnal Green.

Young and Willmott had commented unfavourably on the consequences of wholesale clearance; although in his subsequent study of Dagenham, Willmott concluded that 'many of the migrants to Dagenham and their children have settled and built in the new district a life which, in its social organisation, is very like the old ... it is the resilience of these familiar forms of solidarity amongst the people of Dagenham which is, above all, so impressive.' In other words, community can survive the geographical location to which it was originally linked.

Findings similar to those of Willmott and Young in Bethnal Green from other studies [12] have helped to reinforce the influence of the notion of 'community', which continues to the present day. In North Kensington the Greater London Council is tackling an urban renewal project in an area so dense with 'community' that the local housing authority (the Royal Borough of Kensington and Chelsea) felt they could not handle it themselves. In this area, innumerable groups, some of whom claim to be separate 'communities'—e.g. the West Indians—and others who claim to have special insight into the 'community' of North Kensington—e.g. community workers—have been invited to participate in the renewal process so that not only does the 'community' have a say in its future, but in so doing actually develops itself as a 'community' [13]. (As far as the planners are concerned, they want to ensure that those who wish to stay in the area can.)

But it is not only the planners who have been influenced by the community studies; there is strong evidence that the public—of all classes—have accepted them too, and the newspapers, ranging from the *Sunday People* to the *Sunday Times*, are full of stories which refer to the urban 'community' as an accepted fact. 'Coronation Street', television's longest running soap opera, is about, and based on, urban folklore. There is no doubt that in the urban public's mind, the picture revealed by studies like Young and Willmott's is close to their own experience: while the concept of the urban village may be far more complex than its cosy ring implies, nevertheless it holds a grain of truth. However, before accepting both the power of the concept of 'community' and the persuasiveness of its studies and coming under their joint influence, it would be prudent to examine the strand in British urban sociology that appears to stand in contradiction to 'community'.

The 'rough/respectable' dichotomy

It may seem strange to claim this dichotomy for British *urban* sociology since the heterogeneity of the working class in terms of aspirations, values, behaviour patterns, and ascribed status has long been a theme within the entire range of British 'sociologies' [14]. However, it has particular relevance to urban concentrations for two reasons. First, it is a theme that most often arises in discussion of how working-class people behave and perceive other people's behaviour in the context of their *values*. The terms 'rough' and 'respectable' are used by working-class people and sociologists alike as shorthand to denote, amongst other things, what language people use, how their children behave, whether they own certain consumer goods, whether they are spontaneously neighbourly, whether they have net curtains, whether they are in debt, whether they are clean or dirty, whether they make the beds. The point is that the terms are used to describe people at the point of *consumption* rather than the point of production—occupation, as we shall see later, appears to have little to do with the ascription of these terms. The second reason for its particular relevance within urban sociology is as follows: the spatial distribution of 'roughs' and 'respectables' has traditionally been used as a predictor of neighbour relations, for it has been found in a number of studies (some of which are referred to later) that 'respectables' are most likely to choose to have greater interaction with 'respectable' neighbours than with those they consider 'rough'. The concept's most frequent use has been in studies of council estates where neighbours have almost always been unable to choose whom they live next to—and hence sociologists have found these estates a good test-bed for assessing positive or negative reactions of residents to other members of the working class. Moreover, on council estates opportunities to move away, and thereby give physical semblance to the social distance already perceived, are rather constrained. Thus, such studies provide us with graphic pictures of status antagonisms between members of the same class played out in the same locus. The fact that they do all have to live in the same place appears to make the problems worse rather than better, and hence many studies have found large numbers of both 'roughs' and 'respectables' who wish to move away. Thus location has become a very important variable in these studies—both as a more or less controllable test-bed for the sociologists and as a source of some anxiety to the residents.

But the dichotomy is by no means a recent phenomenon: Gareth Stedman-Jones' study of London in the second half of the nineteenth century [15] shows that the upper echelons of the manual working class were well aware of heterogeneity amongst workers—and concerned to maintain social and

physical distance between the different sub-groups they perceived. In their evidence to the 1882 Select Committee on
Artisans' and Labourers' Dwellings Improvement, the Trades
Council suggested that the state build and subsidize suburban
housing for those members of the working class who could afford
to commute; for the poor tied to the centre they recommended
state-built blocks of flats, subsidized by the rates if necessary.
In 1885 the Trades Council produced a fourfold classification
of workers into artisans, labourers, street traders, vagrants and
thieves [16]. They recommended that the state provide three
different types of dwelling for the first three categories, and that
vagrants and thieves should be restricted to common lodging-
houses. Admittedly, there were practical considerations that
helped to explain this suggestion: conflict had arisen between
street traders and people who took in laundry over the use of
water points and it was thought that such conflicts between
different groups of workers would not arise if like kept with like.
It seems strange, however, that rather than suggest piped water
to all dwellings, the Trades Council went to the lengths of
recommending different dwelling types in different locations.

In his notably unsentimental account of a Salford slum at
the turn of the century, Robert Roberts reinforces the point
about the importance of distinctions within the working class.
He writes:

> Socially the unskilled workers and their families who made up about
> fifty per cent of the populations in our industrial cities, varied as
> much from the manual elite as did people in the middle station
> from the aristocracy. Before 1914 skilled workers generally did not
> strive to join a higher rank; they were only too concerned to main-
> tain position within their own stratum. Inside the working class
> there existed, I believe, a stratified form of society whose implica-
> tions and consequences have hardly yet been explored [17].

Half a century later, Leo Kuper, in his study of an inter-war
overspill estate in Coventry, found similar preoccupations with
status [18].

> It would be misleading to assume that, because the residents of
> Braydan Road are predominantly 'working class', they are homo-
> geneous with reference to anything other than occupation. Certainly,
> in relation to our problem, that of neighbouring, representatives of
> the so-called 'working class' express a great variety of attitudes and

moreover they also evaluate their neighbours by criteria which have nothing to do with occupation [19].

He found it possible to divide the eighty-seven respondents into 'rough' and 'respectable' categories by observing housekeeping standards and the use of taboo words. These two categories were useful in predicting friendship categories for, on the whole, like chose like. 'Occupational and income group classifications revealed no pattern in the distribution of choices.' He also found that children were a major source of anxiety about status for two reasons: first, parents worried that children who had not yet learnt the rules of neighbour relations would cause upsets between neighbours, and second, that, as Kuper puts it, their children might get a 'wrong imprint', by 'catching' the habits of the 'rough' children. Indeed the importance of 'catching' manners is so great that Kuper states:

> Conflict arises from the varied status aspirations of residents. The threat of 'rough' manners causes the 'superior' residents to insulate themselves and their children from the polluting contacts, and finally to move out of the area.

So here again we have evidence of working-class sub-groups wishing to move away from each other. Similar evidence of the rough/respectable dichotomy emerged in a study of council estates in Liverpool and Sheffield [20] although here there was no documentation of people trying to move away from each other. On the other hand, it was again found that children were a source of anxiety—since they symbolized both how successful parents were in forcing or persuading children to conform to their valued behaviour patterns, and also how successful parents *might* be as far as aspirations for their children's future were concerned.

It would, however, be wrong to infer that 'respectables' are necessarily aspirant. Josephine Klein makes an important distinction between people who wish to *maintain* standards and thus differentiate themselves from the 'roughs' and others, whom she terms 'status dissenters', who aspire to 'a materially richer, socially more ambitious, more open, freer way of life' [21]. 'Respectables' in older areas can be described as 'traditional', although on new estates she argues that they would be defined

as 'rough' within that more competitive context. Thus it does
not necessarily follow from being labelled 'respectable' that such
a family would wish to move away from an older urban area—
indeed, the reverse may be true. However when they perceive
an area to be *changing* in such a way that they can no longer
maintain original or 'traditional' standards—particularly with
regard to the manners of their children—this may be regarded
as a very great incentive to move away. This point about how
the changing nature of the Inner City persuades the traditionally
'respectable' but not necessarily aspirant to leave is one to which
we shall return later in this book, for it throws a great deal of
light on our survey evidence.

The suburbs

The question of what kind of people leave the City leads
naturally to the supplementary issue of their destination when
they leave. This, in turn, helps to identify the third thread in
our discussion—the significance of suburbia. British attitudes to
the City and its place in our culture have always been ambiva-
lent, as Raymond Williams (among others) has demonstrated
in *The Country and the City* [22]. Indeed, Asa Briggs has suggested,
perhaps not entirely seriously, that anti-urban sentiment in this
country goes back to the Romans [23]. Resistance to the process
of urbanization has been strong; but there has often been more
than a trace of artificiality in it—the country as a kind of Eden,
seen dimly through rose-coloured spectacles. Access to this
Arcady is limited—apart from the ritual yokels—to the happy
few; those for whom, as Harold Macmillan is supposed to have
said when helping to commit his country to the Suez adventure,
the lawns of England have to be kept green.

Yet, in the real world, England experienced under the impact
of the Industrial Revolution the earliest and most complete shift
from a predominantly rural to an urban society; so complete,
indeed, that by 1891, 72 per cent of the population lived in cities,
whose steady growth had continued almost unchecked throughout the nineteenth century. The capacity of these cities, in the
absence of external constraints, to spread out geographically,
had an incidentally important consequence in ensuring that the
English (unlike the Scots or French) developed no tradition of
flat living.

Against this background, suburbia can be seen as an attempt to recapture the imagined delights of the country without sacrificing the present benefits of the city; it is, in R. E. Pahl's classical formulation, *urbs in rure*. At first, the suburbs were mainly the prerogative of the prosperous, as they have been in most civilizations—though this did not protect them from the scorn of the aesthetes. Ruskin, in a passage in *Sesame and Lilies* [24] later used as an epigraph by Ebenezer Howard, appeals for new houses that will be built 'strongly, beautifully, and in groups of limited extent; kept in proportion to their streams and walled round, so that there may be no festering and wretched suburb anywhere, but clear and busy street within and the open country without.'

But when, towards the end of the nineteenth century, cheap travel became more generally available, the attractions of suburbia proved to extend across social classes. As Sir Frederic Osborn put it in his *Green Belt Cities* [25]

> What did the internal combustion engine and the electric motor do but vastly enlarge the noble company of carriage-folk? The tram, the bus, the train, the tube, enabled millions to seek the eternally desired situation between town and country.

But the benefits of this increased mobility were not evenly spread. David Thorns, commenting on the process in his study of suburbia, observes that it was initiated by the middle class and that

> ... the image which these suburbs held was, therefore, largely a middle class one. This meant that a move to the suburb was seen as a requirement of the working class man who desired to be socially mobile. The working class man who had heightened social aspirations was the one most anxious to take up suburban residence [26].

The working-class suburbs of London, which were made possible by the introduction of cheap workman's fares towards the end of the century, were the tangible evidence that the working classes could escape from the Inner City—although the poor quality of the speculatively built housing in which they often had to live was part of the price that they paid. Then, early in the twentieth century, local authorities began to become involved in the provision of cheap rented housing on the outskirts of cities but to better standards—the London County Council at St Helier and Becontree, for example, or Manchester at Wythenshaw. In this way, opportunities for housing in the suburbs that satisfied the middle-class ideal were nevertheless made accessible, through the operation of housing subsidies, to a few of the urban working class. We examine this development in far more detail in the following chapter; suffice it to say here that the 'pull' of the suburbs has been a strong theme in British urban history, and, at the same time, the mediation, by public bodies, of opportunities to live in suburban environments a very important aspect of the development, in the twentieth century, of state intervention.

Urban managerialism

A fourth strand in British urban studies, of more recent vintage than the community studies, is that known as the 'urban managerialist thesis' [27]. The relevance of this thesis for our study lies chiefly in the fact that it is resource-centred. We are here concerned with a particular resource—the housing and environment of New and Expanding Towns—which is allocated through a particularly complex system. The urban managerialist thesis helps to crystallize the main issues, which can be stated in the form of a question: who allocates what to whom, how, and in whose interests?

However, one of the problems about using the thesis for our purposes, is that it is at an early stage of development and hence in a state of flux. Moreover, few pieces of empirical work have appeared that are analysed within its framework and none of them had been published when we undertook this study; this study did not, therefore, originally establish hypotheses drawn from its ideas, and an attempt to use the framework for parts of this book is something of a leap from nothing concrete into the unknown. Nevertheless, it would be foolish to ignore the thesis since it raises so many interesting questions about the nature of New Towns policy, both as that policy has been conceived theoretically and as it has worked out in practice.

The most developed statement of the thesis is in the second edition of R. E. Pahl's collection of essays *Whose City?* [28]. In that book, he suggests four models of resource control and allocation which might provide the answers to the question we have posed: 'Who allocates what, how, to whom, and in whose interests?' The '"*pure" managerialist model*' posits that control rests solely with the professional officers concerned—hence, allocation will presumably be in the interests of those professions, as they interpret them. Any conflict will be inter-professional. The '*statist model*' 'assumes that control over local resources and facilities is primarily a matter for the national government and that local professionals or managers have very little room for manoeuvre.' Thus allocation will presumably depend on how the national government sees its interests or ideology best served—and, ultimately, government will probably act in such a way as to retain its power. The locus of conflict will be within national government—between civil servants and politicians, and between politicians of different brands. The third model posits '*control-by-capitalists*'. 'This assumes that at either national or local levels resources are allocated primarily to service the interests of private capitalists.' Thus, as Pahl puts it 'At a local level private profit is a more legitimate basis for the allocation of, say, central locations than public good.' The role of government, both local and national, is presumably to maximize the resources available and any conflict will be between capitalists in the scramble to make the most of those resources. The '*pluralist model*' 'assumes a permanent tension between national bureaucracies, committed to obtaining and distributing larger resources (following partly their own internal logic of growth), and the interests of private capital manifested through the economic pressures of "the City", private industry and the political party representing the dominant class.' Here, conflict is part of the model itself; different public and private interests negotiate for position, and the situation is inherently changeable. It may be possible, at any one point in time, to say in whose interests a particular policy is intended to and actually does operate, but at any moment, unlike with the other models, the situation can change.

Each of these models indicates, therefore, a different set of allocators and interests. The allocators can range from professionals to captains of industry or ministers of state—or all of them: and, depending on which model we adopt, the nature of the interests served by any particular policy alters. As far as New Towns policy is concerned, both the questions and the models raise central questions. If we take the '"pure" managerialist thesis', for example, we can suggest that the professionals and managers within the New Towns process do, indeed, wield power, but that those managers are divided amongst themselves and each grouping acts in its own interests. Thus, we might find that managers in exporting authorities attempt to reduce the outflow of industry if that outflow adversely affects their economic base, while New Town development corporation managers may attempt to 'net' the most successful firms they can in order to maintain the growth and 'success' of their New Towns. Similarly, housing managers of exporting authorities may seek to reduce their own 'problems' by ridding themselves of the homeless and the one-parent families, while the New Towns may strenuously resist receiving such new and 'non-respectable' residents. If this view of the situation is accepted, it is not easy to see either capitalism or the national government as the main agents of policy and policy change. Policy is subject to negotiations between groups of managers working within separate bureaucracies.

Similarly, it can also be argued that the 'statist model' has considerable relevance to New Towns policy. For it is normally in the interests of a democratically elected national government to ensure that goods and resources can be seen to be distributed more or less equitably over space; it is important to ensure, for example, that a worker in a car factory in Liverpool has more or less the same income and life chance as a similar worker in Luton—otherwise both nationally negotiated wages policies and a consistent level of political support are difficult to achieve. At the same time, national government has to ensure that the actions of local government do not distort national efforts towards equity and 'territorial justice'. As far as New Towns are concerned, they can be seen, therefore, as part of a national effort to resolve, through overspill policies, some of the locality-specific problems of urbanization, and, at the same time, alleviate the problems of regional economic imbalance through the concentration of growth in the New Towns which, it is hoped, will act as economic multipliers. In this case, national government can be seen to pursue the twin goals of urban overspill and economic equity between regions; local government and New Town development corporations simply execute these policies. Thus, according to this model, bargaining at local level over how far the policy should cater for either overspill or

growth pole needs merely amounts to an interpretation of nationally laid down policies. The crucial allocators operate at national
level, and the resources they allocate go both to those in housing
'need' in overcrowded cities, and to the unemployed workers
in the less well-off authorities and regions.

The 'control-by-capitalists' model is one that has been specifically applied to the New Towns. Manuel Castells suggests that
the entire policy was

> a response to the urban crisis in the London region, whose origin
> is to be found in the over-concentration of industry produced by
> the technical and economic development of English Capitalism....
> The individual interest of each firm, seeking to maximize its profits
> is (thus) in contradiction with the equilibrium of the whole, in that
> such a spatial concentration of activity, left to itself, produces a whole
> series of contradictions within the urban system of the London region,
> while at the same time accentuating the imbalance between regions
> [29].

Thus, he argues, central government intervened to regroup
industry in a way that gave firms collectively more opportunity
to grow. But as is the nature of the creature capitalism, its fatal
flaws were only temporarily assuaged, and 'all the problems re-
appeared still more acutely' during the 1960s. The argument
is, then, that the original conception of the New Towns policy
fits this model. It might also be suggested that the actual *operation*
of the policy fits it as well. It is clear that the system of incentives provided for firms to move, involving removal grants and
the provision of relatively cheap all-found factory accommodation in the New Towns, is a handsome resource for private
industry; it is also clear, as we shall see in later chapters, that
policies for allocating New Town housing are geared to the needs
of industry, in the sense that Development Corporation dwellings
for rent are almost entirely restricted to those who have jobs
in the New Towns' firms. Since, on the whole, only those who
constitute 'suitable *labour*' (as opposed to suitable *tenants*) are
able to move to a New Town, it is a moot point—and one we
shall return to frequently—as to whether national or local
government intentions to use New Towns as a means of allevi-
ating housing need can ever counterbalance the needs of industry
for particular kinds of labour. It is another moot point as to
whether the predominance of the needs of industry in planned

migration is a particular feature of capitalism (it is, for example, a very common feature of Eastern European 'socialism'); nevertheless, it is clear that where relatively cheap and accessible resources of plant and labour are made available by the State, firms intent on maximizing profit are likely to look very seriously at the possibilities of using those resources.

Since we have suggested that all three models so far discussed have much relevance to New Town policy, it might seem that the last—the 'pluralist model'—is the most suitable of all, since its name implies that it covers all contingencies. In fact, however, it seems that the pluralist model probably has the least direct relevance to New Towns policy, since it posits continuous competition and tension between three types of institution: 'national bureaucracies', 'private capital' and 'local authorities'. This is probably not a suitable way of analysing New Towns policy; it is more relevant to state that the policy is characterized by tension between at least three types of *goal*, which are mediated by institutions of all three kinds. These goals are: regional equity, reduction of urban densities, and provision for people in housing 'need'. Such goals are in considerable conflict, as we shall see later in this book; the process of achieving them involves national and local governments and private capital, sometimes in unison and sometimes in conflict.

Since we have already indicated that our initial hypotheses were not framed in the context of the urban managerialist thesis, we make no claims to the adoption of these models in the chapters that follow, or to any systematic testing of their validity. However, the general perspective that derives from the thesis is useful in considering the material that we gathered in the course of our study, because it helps to focus attention on some of the key issues. In particular, the identification of the beneficiaries of New and Expanding Towns policies is of concern to us. In reviewing the material, we will therefore have particular regard to the implications of the question posed earlier: who allocates what, to whom, how and in whose interests?

At this stage in the discussion, some explanation of the origins of the New Towns that grew out of Howard's original concept is essential. Our analysis will not be clear without some understanding of what the originators of this unique (though by now widely imitated) social experiment were trying to achieve. But, perhaps still more important, the ways in which their original intentions have been translated into action have had a decisive influence on the extent to which the New Towns (and the Expanding Towns subsequently created as a supplementary device to the same end) have succeeded in contributing towards the solution of the problems that Howard himself identified as central—those of the Inner City and its inhabitants.

References

1. FILKIN, C. and LAMBERT, J., *Race*, Vol. 12, No. 3, January 1971.
2. See, for example, YOUNG, M. and WILLMOTT, P., *Family and Kinship in East London* (Routledge and Kegan Paul, 1957) and WILLMOTT, P. and YOUNG, M., *Family and Class in a London Suburb* (Routledge and Kegan Paul, 1960).
3. BELL, COLIN and NEWBY, HOWARD, *Community Studies; an introduction to the Sociology of the local community* (George Allen and Unwin, 1971).
4. BELL and NEWBY, op. cit., p. 26.
5. See, for example, MITCHELL, C. D. et al., *Neighbourhood and Community: an inquiry into social relationships on housing estates in Liverpool and Sheffield* (University of Liverpool Press, 1954) and KUPER, LEO (ed.), 'Blueprint for Living Together', *Living in Towns* (The Cresset Press, 1953).
6. YOUNG and WILLMOTT, op. cit.
7. YOUNG and WILLMOTT, op. cit., p. 113.
8. and 9. YOUNG and WILLMOTT, op. cit., p. 186.
10. GANS, HERBERT, *The Urban Villagers: group and class in the life of Italian-Americans* (Free Press, 1962).
11. TAYLOR, NICHOLAS, *The Village in the City* (Maurice Temple Smith in association with New Society, 1973), p. 212.
12. See, for example, DENNIS, NORMAN, *People and Planning* (Faber and Faber, 1970) and DENNIS, NORMAN, *Public Participation and Planners' Blight* (Faber and Faber, 1972).
13. REDPATH, R. and CHILVERS, D. J., 'Swinbrook: a community study applied' in *Greater London Quarterly Bulletin*, No. 26, March 1974.
14. See, for example, KLEIN, JOSEPHINE, *Samples from English Cultures*, pp. 198–201 and 219–69 (Routledge and Kegan Paul, 1965).
15. STEDMAN-JONES, G., *Outcast London* (Clarendon Press, 1971).
16. Trades Council evidence to 1885 Royal Commission on the Housing of the Working Classes. Quoted in STEDMAN-JONES, G., op. cit., p. 227.
17. ROBERTS, R., *The Classic Slum* (Penguin Books, 1973), p. 13.
18. KUPER, LEO (ed.), op. cit.
19. KUPER, LEO (ed.), op. cit., p. 67.
20. MITCHELL, C. D. et al., op. cit.
21. KLEIN, JOSEPHINE, op. cit., p. 241.
22. WILLIAMS, RAYMOND, *The Country and the City* (Chatto and Windus, 1973).
23. BRIGGS, ASA, *Victorian Cities* (Penguin Books, 1968), p. 72.
24. RUSKIN, JOHN, *Sesame and Lilies* (Dent, 1907).

25. OSBORN, FREDERIC J., *Green Belt Cities* (Faber and Faber, 1946).

26. THORNS, DAVID, *Suburbia* (Paladin Books, 1973).

27. See, for example, PAHL, R. E., 'Urban Managerialism reconsidered' in PAHL, R. E., *Whose City?* (Penguin, 1975).

28. PAHL, R. E. op. cit., and NORMAN, PETER, '*Managerialism—a review of recent work*'—paper given at Centre for Environmental Studies Conference on Urban Change and Conflict, University of York, 1975.

29. CASTELLS, MANUEL, *La Question Urbaine*, translated by Chris Pickvance (Manspero, Paris, 1972), pp. 345–54.

Chapter Two

Suburbia and New Towns: choosing a destination

The Concept of the New Towns

Ebenezer Howard saw the problem of the nineteenth-century city as a physical one, to be solved by physical means. The New Town, as he originally conceived it, was the apotheosis of the suburb, but radically transformed in the process of its elevation into a new environment for family living, at low density, self-contained but of strictly limited size, protected by a strict system of control over land use, furnished with its own access to employment. As such, it was to be sharply distinguished from ordinary suburban developments—as, indeed, its chief protagonists struggled scrupulously to do for decades, dismissing as fraudulent all variations on the orthodox suburban theme from the highest—Bedford Park or Hampstead Garden Suburb—to the lowest speculative development at the end of a railway line in Metroland, for all the world like patent medicine salesmen exhorting the public to accept no substitute. Their product had to be a new form of urban entity: the Social City.

The essence of Howard's case is contained in his famous concept of the 'third magnet'—the Garden City as the combination of the attractions of the city and those of the country. If this third magnet could be created, then 'the migration to the towns—the old, crowded, chaotic slum towns of the past—will be effectively checked, and the current of population set in precisely the opposite direction—to the New Towns, bright and fair, wholesome and beautiful' [1]. If London, to which Howard devotes particular attention in *Garden Cities of Tomorrow*, could be demagnetized in this way, the consequences for the housing conditions of the city would be of the very greatest importance. With the fall in population 'obviously, house-property in London will fall in rental value, and fall enormously. Slum property will sink to zero, and the whole working population will move into houses of a class quite above those which they can now afford to occupy' [2].

Although Howard's conclusions about the consequences of a falling population proved to rest on a very shaky basis, his concern with the question of the implications of dispersal for the cities themselves forms another important theme—though one to which less attention was paid in the subsequent debate [3]. Howard himself indicates quite clearly that this wider problem, though central to the argument that he advances, must await the solution of the immediate difficulty—the creation of a single Garden City 'as a working model' [4], to demonstrate in tangible form the virtues of a planned community.

Howard's own determination to conduct that experiment—and his good fortune in convincing a number of 'men of standing and experience in practical affairs' [5] to collaborate with him, produced the Letchworth experiment. First Garden City Limited was set up in 1903, as a private business venture. As such, the town that was eventually constructed differed in several important respects from subsequent New Towns. The approach adopted embodied two of the essential principles in Howard's original conception—collective control of the entire site, and economic self-containment. But the need to attract private investment led to concessions on the design of housing, though Howard's guiding principle of low densities was adhered to firmly enough. Letchworth also attracted a minority of eccentrics, whose appearance was of some significance, in helping to perpetuate the tinge of crankiness that clung to the Garden City movement from the outset, and took a long time to dispel.

If at Letchworth, as Jane Jacobs suggests, Howard 'defined wholesome housing in terms only of suburban physical qualities and small-town social qualities' [6] it was because the failure of urban housing, cast in a very different mould, was self-evident in the London of the early twentieth century. Moreover, as Osborn points out, the generally recognized goals of public housing policy were pitched in precisely those terms: as the Government department then responsible for housing put it in

1919, 'it must be borne in mind that (tenement) dwellings are opposed to the habits and traditions of our people, that they are condemned by the best housing experience, and that, as already stated, where tenements have generally prevailed, opinion is steadily becoming opposed to them' [7]. And indeed those model tenements provided by an earlier generation of housing reformers to meet the needs of the urban working class had demonstrably failed—a failure dramatized, in London, by the pressures brought about by the most intensive migration that this country has ever experienced, the exodus of Jewish refugees from the pogroms of Tsarist Russia. But if the failures were evident to commentators of every shade of opinion from Jack London to General Booth, the solutions were less evident.

However, planned dispersal, in one form or another, had always figured among the range of possibilities that were canvassed. The LCC's own analysis of the housing problems of the working class (1913) pointed in this direction. Although the authority itself possessed only a pale shadow of the powers that it was later to obtain and could do comparatively little to promote the process, the Council nevertheless concluded from the evidence available to it that the processes of voluntary migration were likely to increase and that policy should be adapted in consequence. 'Future action,' the authors of the report suggested, 'should take the form, as a preliminary, of careful and periodic inquiries into the movement of the population and the demands for labour in order to keep in touch with, and to follow with appropriate measures, any alterations which may appear. If the existing conditions are maintained, housing and accommodation can be provided most usefully and economically on the outskirts of the county or in extra-London districts.... New accommodation, publicly provided, should be suitable for the less fortunate and should therefore not contain on average more than three or four rooms, while the rent should be the lowest which would recoup the outlay. Cheap tenements in the less central districts are of no use to the working classes, unless there are adequate means of locomotion at convenient times and reasonable fares. The provision of accommodation must therefore be combined with unremitting efforts to secure such means of locomotion' [8].

In due course, the success of Letchworth and its viability as an alternative solution to these problems became evident—

though it was a long time before the parent company became so profitable as to provoke an attempted takeover of the company by speculators, which was only thwarted by the promotion of private legislation. This success (later reinforced by that of a second experiment at Welwyn) was of particular significance, in that it provided tangible evidence of the viability of the New Towns concept at a time when an opportunity arose to interest central government in that concept.

In this changed climate of opinion, and with the increased attention being paid to the housing problem and the potentiality for increased State intervention—a concern underlined by Lloyd George's promise to provide the returning soldiers with 'homes fit for heroes'—the Garden City movement had a strong case to make, and the existence of Letchworth made it stronger. When a group of younger propagandists advanced the case in *New Towns after the War* (1918) for a hundred satellite Garden Cities, they were able to do so in terms that were not Utopian, but soberly realistic. For the striking thing about the propaganda of the Garden City Association (which brought together Howard and a group of younger supporters) was that it rested on secure foundations; the proven failure of existing policy, and the demonstrably intense pressure on the heavily congested inner city areas. Yet the final achievement of their goal of official involvement had to wait for another thirty years and a second World War before finally being achieved. Until then the Garden City movement remained an intriguing eddy in the current of new thinking about the future of English cities, but one with no direct influence on the outcome, in terms of official policy.

The Expansion of Suburbia

Throughout the period before Howard's ideas finally reached fruition, London's suburban expansion continued unchecked. With housing costs at their lowest level ever, in relation to incomes, it was possible in the middle thirties to buy a suburban semi with a deposit as low as £20 and at a total cost of under £500. Planning restrictions were still virtually non-existent and 'the devasting onrush of the speculative builder' as Professor William Robson described it, in his evidence to the Barlow Commission, which no local authority 'even pretended to regulate and guide for the common good' [9] surged on. But among those carried out to the suburban pastures described in affectionate detail in Alan A. Jackson's *Semi-Detached London* [10] were large numbers of members of the respectable working class, anxious to seize for their own families the opportunity for a place in the sun, combining both amenity and status. For the suburbs became heavily loaded with 'respectable' symbolism— as a typical advertisement for suburban semis round London, newly built in the 1930s, made clear:

> Nouveau Homes are offered to families of good breeding who wish to acquire a house to be proud of at a cost of less than £1 a week [11]

But the symbols of the suburbs have been far more complex than this advertisement would imply—not merely a visible badge of social success, or the places where people of 'good breeding' could congregate to do 'well-bred' things together. R. E. Pahl summarizes other aspects of human life, organization and values which the suburbs or what he calls, the 'fringe' can represent:

> Maybe the familism and search for community involved in the centrifugal movement is a tacit revolt against industrial society. The flight from the city may be a folk movement away from its dirt, violence, and racial and religious tensions. The pastoral image of green fields, small community and basic privacy of family relation-ships may draw people away from the larger problems of the metropolis to the more manageable world of the fringe [12].

All these themes deserve further exploration, since they may help to explain not merely the movement from the City, but also its composition and direction. The first important theme is what Pahl calls the 'more manageable world of the fringe'. The theme of control: self-control, control of one's immediate surroundings—through management of one's own domestic internal and open space, thence control of one's family's activities as they work and play, political control through combination with other like-minded citizens, the sheer orderliness of streets planned as unities—can be contrasted with a more anarchic and yet, ironically, to many, less *free* image of the City. For the suburbs can be said to be physical embodiment of the virtues

of the 'property-owning democracy': they allow for freedom
frcm interference by traffic, noise, other children (because you
can keep your own in your own garden and others out by means
of a fence and a gate), and nosy neighbours. Thus some of the
kinds of control one can have in the suburbs over one's own
environment are also an assertion of individual freedom, for it
is in the cities that unpredictable interference from traffic, noise,
neighbours, other people's children, occurs.

Yet the City contains a potential for different kinds of life style
and politics which some will find pleasantly anarchic and others
repulsively anomic. Gareth Stedman-Jones says of London
in the 1860s to 1880s that it 'was haunted by the spectre of
Parisian barricades' [13]. To some, such an idea would hardly
be a 'spectre'—it would be a vision. But to others it would be
reason enough to flee to the suburbs; as Ruth Glass puts it, when
describing anti-urbanism in the nineteenth century:

> The more the towns were deserted by the upper and middle classes,
> the more plainly were they also the barracks of a vast working
> class whose lessons in the power of combination had already begun,
> and whose sporadic riots were portents of latent insurrection ... the
> memory of this fear has continued to be a reason for British
> antipathy against urbanism [14].

For those to whom political control was a key factor, there were
both a push and a pull factor: the fear of losing control of events
served as the push, while the hope of retrieving it elsewhere,
in the new environment, acted as the pull. For others, the com-
pensating attractions of the City continued to be greater. Apart
from the familiarity of the existing situation and the accessibility
of work, the City has other qualities which have always made
it a magnet for newcomers: it is the centre of events, political,
social and cultural; it provides variety and excitement. Often
it is also a shelter—a source of welcome anonymity, an opportunity to begin again.

It may, indeed, be possible to generalize about the *type* of
person to whom the unpredictable excitement of the City is particularly appealing and in contrast, about those to whom it is
particularly repulsive. There are obviously those who find the
potential political ferment of the City attractive for ideological
reasons: they either wish to promote it or learn how to control

it. Either way, the challenge is exciting and exacting. Then there are those who take a transitional view of City life; they may be well-heeled enough to know they can move away if things get too unpleasant, or they may be young enough to regard this period of their lives as a transitional one—meantime they can take advantage of the multiple choices of politics and life-style available in cities.

In contrast, those repelled by multiplicity of choices, or the frustration of not being able to exercise them, are likely to be of two kinds. First there will be those on low incomes who cannot use what they see around them, or who may be repelled by inherent uncertainties and cannot regard their present life as one over which they have control, since they have not got the financial resources to move elsewhere. Then there are house-holds with dependants—very old or very young—where the middle-aged adults may feel that their dependants are incapable of coping with the stresses and strains of City life. These are the people to whom the prospect of control, rigidities, rules and regulations are likely to be attractive—and hence, for them, the appeal of the suburbs. Thus fear of the City—or its obverse, excitement—will repel or attract different people and their particular characteristics are likely to be age- or income-related. For those repelled by it, the neatness and apparent conformity of the suburbs appear particularly attractive.

But there is another image of the suburb which stands in contrast to this image of order: its romanticism. Dyos has actually gone as far as to say that the suburb 'is the unanswerable argu-ment in favour of the romanticism of the Englishman' [15]. He implies that the suburb is the poor man's substitute for the rural idyll—and that this idyll is a romantic one. Ruth Glass takes a more cynical line and suggests that the suburbs are nothing more than imitative snobbery:

> If the peerage and squirearchy were inaccessible there were still their many imitations all down the social scale: those who could not reach the Manor House could always retreat to the stronghold of a sub-urban villa or, at least, to a semi-detached jerry built, mock Tudor *mon repos* [16].

She suggests that it is not what Pahl calls 'the pastoral image of green fields' that suburbanites seek—rather the thrill of being *almost* like their betters, who happen to be able to afford green fields. Also, if romanticism stands for wildness, strong feeling, unpredictability, volatility, then neither the country seat nor *mon repos* qualify, for their common denominator is order. The image is not so much 'green fields' but rather green fields with well-placed copses, artificial lakes, gazebos and follies. Their real life counterparts are the herbaceous borders, rose bushes, gnomes with fishing rods and garden sheds of Edgware and Crawley. This is 'pretend country', as far removed from the true country as black is from white. The pastoral image is far more complex than it seems at first and related less to simple images of the windswept countryside than to order and snobbery. As Glass argues, it has a harder, more worldly gloss to it than 'romanticism' would imply. However—and here is the important point about the relationship between suburbs and the country—there is no doubt that easy access to the 'real' countryside from the country seat or the Edwardian suburb is both important and simple. It is a place to take the children for a walk, the dog for a romp and one's lover for a kiss and a cuddle. The concept is simple, because it is not muddled by the idea of ownership, let alone control. The countryside as an accessible place *symbolizes* nothing—it is simply a good place to be, especially when the sun shines.

New and Expanding Towns: the development of planned migration

New Towns, at one level, represent an opportunity to make these pleasures associated with the suburbs more widely accessible. At another, they epitomize order, a taming of nature by the planner. Not for nothing did they provide the much praised keystone of the structure of the post-Second World War planning system.

As for so many social reforms, war provided the catalyst that brought together the different streams of thinking within the framework of analysis provided by the Barlow Commission's Report. This Royal Commission, which had reported in 1940, arrived at three basic conclusions: first, that continued congestion of urban areas was harmful on economic, social and strategic grounds; second, that there was a need for the establishment of a policy of dispersal of both industry and population from congested urban areas, particularly London, and finally, that a reasonable balance of industrial development (with respect to size and variety) throughout all regions in Great Britain should be encouraged. The stress on the need for the reorganization of congested areas lent impetus to urban renewal programmes of later years; the recommendation for decentralization laid the foundation for the policy of dispersal; and the need for a balance in industrial development between the regions provided the starting point for policies of regional planning and development.

The Barlow report represents a decisive turning point in the evolution of the New Towns movement and, indeed, of planning in Britain. In essence, the Commissioners had accepted the substance of the case that Howard and his associates had developed, by endorsing their arguments for planned dispersal from major cities.

However, the fact that the New Towns became a key device in a range of broader planning policies also had decisive implications for the type of people for whom they were to cater, and the manner in which they provided for them; and the way in which they were incorporated into these policies has indelibly coloured their subsequent history. In essence, as Ray Thomas comments, 'London's new towns are the product of the policy proposed in Abercrombie's Greater London Plan of 1944' [17] which Sir Frederic Osborn describes as 'the first fully worked out Garden City plan for a great metropolis' [18]. Certainly in physical planning terms, this Plan was the most advanced attempt of its kind, on a regional scale. In developing the basis for the establishment of a policy for dispersal, the authors of the report took the view that no new industries should be allowed to establish themselves in the County of London and its adjoining counties and that regulations for controlling the increase of industrial employment should be instituted; that a number of industries and their personnel should be dispersed; and that new planning organizations should be set up to serve the London region.

One of the most fundamental proposals of the Plan is the 'Zoning of London', based on a system of concentric rings, whereby there would be a series of new towns with a green belt between them and the built-up area of London. Zone one represented the Inner or Central Area of London whose high density made dispersal necessary. Limits would be placed on population density here. Zone two represented the suburbs, with comparatively low-density housing. This zone was to remain stable with respect to housing and industry and also have a limited population density. The third zone represented the green belt (as defined by the Green Belt Act, 1938). Then mainly in agricultural use, this zone was to be used for recreational purposes while retaining its rural character. It was to be free from industrial development and the growth of existing towns and villages around it was to be strictly controlled, to a limit of 300 000 new inhabitants. The fourth zone, beyond the green belt, was to absorb the London population dispersed from the Inner Area. In this zone, the New Towns would be built.

The over-riding aim of Abercrombie's policy of dispersal was the reduction and stabilization of London's population and employment through the creation of these moderate-sized New Towns with a population of about 50 000, on the lines of the Garden Cities originally envisaged by Howard. The decision of the incoming Labour Government in 1945 to appoint a committee of inquiry under Lord Reith provided the clinching evidence of the new Government's intention to act: and, the three reports of Reith's New Towns Committee provide a series of clear-cut statements against which to measure the successes and the failures of subsequent policy.

The task of the Commission, as Lord Reith and his colleagues conceived it, was: 'to conduct an essay in civilization, by seizing an opportunity to design, evolve and carry into execution for the benefit of coming generations the means for a happy and gracious way of life'. This graciousness was to be achieved in two ways. First, by the relief of pressure on existing cities, and especially 'the twin evils of slums and overcrowding'. These, the Committee argued, 'have their roots in the unregulated and excessive growth of towns during a period when the health of the people, no less than their spiritual and social well-being, were sacrificed to industrial progress. Men must live near their work. Yet only in recent years has come a full realisation that the solution of the many problems to which these evils give rise, to say nothing of the spoliation of the countryside by ill-considered building, is by setting some limit to the haphazard spoil of our existing cities and by providing in New Towns, wisely sited and skilfully planned, a proper balance between housing and industry.' In addition, such New Towns should necessarily be socially as well as economically balanced. For 'New Towns that are to be developed as "self-contained and balanced communities" are the antithesis of the dormitory suburb. One of their primary purposes is to provide for the overspill of industry and population as the congested areas of our great cities are cleared and rebuilt in lower densities; another is to regroup persons from areas of diminishing population and from small scattered communities whose major industry is declining, and to rehouse them, not merely with greater amenities, but in proper relation to newly established industries' [19].

This is clearly a formidable undertaking and one cast in the form of a moral imperative characteristic of the Committee's Chairman. 'In making such an attempt,' the Committee comments, 'we are fully sensible of the magnitude of the responsibility placed upon us which far exceeds the mere devising of machinery for the ordered laying of bricks and mortar.' Such an approach also involves very broad claims indeed for the efficacy of New Towns policy, and it would be fair to add that the proposals of the two further reports that followed the first report of the Committee do not fully measure up to such heroic aspirations. Among the passages of particular interest are those which lay stress on the positive functions of the New Towns—to serve not as a rehousing area in connection with slum clearance, but as a planned entity incorporating 'the best possible social and economic balance'. At the same time, the Committee recognized that the viability of the New Towns would depend on providing sufficient employment for a disparate population. But they added: 'beyond that point the problem is not economic at all nor even a vaguely social one; it is, to be frank, one of class distinction. So far as these distinctions are based on income, taxation and high cost of living are reducing them. We realise also that there are some who would have us ignore their existence. But the problem remains and must be faced; if the community is to be truly balanced, as long as social classes exist all must be represented in it' [20].

The legislation which enabled the New Towns programme to be set in motion was introduced even before the Reith Committee had completed its deliberations. It provided for the

establishment of a separate development corporation for each
town, under an independent chairman—the purpose being as
the Minister responsible later put it, to obtain 'originality of
ideas and experimentation' [21]. In general, the Act proved to
be remarkably well-drafted; Wyndham Thomas comments in
the Town and Country Planning Association's commemorative
volume that 'the New Towns Act is a wonderfully complete and
flexible piece of legislation, and the single-minded development
corporation an inherently effective instrument of public purpose'
[22]. But the overall context within which the eight London
New Towns eventually designated under the Act were intended
to fit had changed almost as soon as the Act was passed. In
the early 1940s, it had been supposed that the birth-rate would
continue to decline, and that one of the long-term difficulties
facing the post-war planners would be population stagnation,
if not outright decline. Even so, the Greater London Plan had
envisaged the planned movement of one million people from
the County of London, and the inner ring, and that the New
Towns would eventually take up to half this overspill. In
practice, the population of the region began to increase at an
unexpectedly rapid rate as the birth-rate turned upwards after
the war, and the major role initially envisaged for the New
Towns as the centrepiece in a planned dispersal policy failed
to materialize. Instead, these broader goals were first blurred
by the initial teething problems encountered by the newly
fledged development corporations, as they struggled to launch
the New Towns in a situation of acute shortages and competition for scarce resources, and then submerged—albeit only
temporarily—by the unplanned growth of population. The
infant New Towns had to survive as best they could as individual
exercises in planned development.

The passage of the Town Development Act in 1952 did imply
a continued commitment to the principle of decentralization.
This legislation set up alternative overspill machinery, by which
development could be undertaken in suitable towns outside the
major conurbations, with Exchequer assistance, but with the
initiative left to the local authorities, and more specifically to
the prospective 'receiving' authority—the Expanding Town. In
the case of London, the scheme could then be implemented either
by the receiving authority itself undertaking the work, with
financial assistance from the LCC (later GLC), or through the

LCC undertaking the work on an agency basis.

However, under the Conservative Government elected in 1951, the current had begun to flow against centralized planning, and although the London New Towns had originally been conceived as an essential part of the regrouping of the population and not merely an exercise in planning for its own sake the instruments essential for the carrying out of such a policy were lacking.

In 1959, the LCC tried to break through the Government's refusal to designate any further New Towns by promoting one themselves, at Hook in Hampshire, but the Government refused the essential financial support, and in Edward Carter's poignant phrase 'the town died in the LCC's womb' [23]. But in 1961 there was an abrupt reversal in Government policy. Not merely had the intensity of the continuing crisis in housing, especially in London, been belatedly borne in on the Government, leading to the passage of the Housing Act of 1961; concern with the country's poor economic performance had led to a resurrection of the whole concept of central planning. The Government that had announced four years earlier than no further New Towns would be designated proceeded to designate five, and to invite the established London New Towns to review their positions, with a view to the possibility of further expansion [24].

For it had become clear, beyond reasonable dispute, that the 'Mark I' New Towns were a success. They had weathered criticism both aesthetic—their alleged embodiment of the concept of 'prairie planning'—and social—the much-touted 'New Towns blues'—and settled down to become places demonstrably attractive to a considerable range of people as places to live in. This success had been due, at least in part, to their conformity to Howard's principle of low densities—which, as David Thorns pointed out, has also, paradoxically, been 'the major stimulus to the growth of the one thing Howard most wanted to prevent, the suburb' [25].

The New Towns and Suburbia: attraction and reaction

How far can the attraction that New Towns now manifestly exercise be distinguished from that of the suburbs generally? After all, as Clawson and Hall emphasize, 'New Towns are supposed to be an alternative to suburbia, not a superior form of it' [26]. Yet, if we take Ruth Glass' point about a 'chain reaction of social imitation' then one can argue that the New Towns are, in their attraction at any rate, another form of suburb—though this was far from being the intention of those who laboured devotedly to launch them. They are a step 'up' in terms of social status, for those unable to afford either a privately built suburban semi or a decent privately owned or rented flat or house in the Inner City. They would also be, if Ruth Glass is right, a step 'up' for the Inner City council tenant who lives in a block of flats—for she would presumably claim that the image of the house with the garden in a New Town is just that bit nearer to the ultimate image of the country seat. But it is by no means entirely a question of status seeking. As we have suggested, the theme of fear of the City is a strong one, and there is no reason why people who move to a New or Expanding Town should not feel that fear, as strongly as those who move to the suburbs. Moreover, the control that they can operate over their immediate surroundings is greater in New Towns than in cities. They can, for example, allow the children to play outside without constant anxiety that they will be run over. They can also choose whether to let their children out at all—since the children can always play in their private garden. They can have more control over which children their own children play with. They can choose for themselves whether to keep the garden neat, and what to grow in it, rather than be subject to the whims of a private or public landlord, or, worse still, not have a garden at all. They can keep a pet without necessarily annoying the neighbours or the landlord. All in all, the vicissitudes of some aspects of their lives are more subject to their control.

However, the second major point to make about suburbs and New Towns is that if one thinks of them purely as symbols rather than good things in themselves as commentators on 'the suburbs' have tended to do, then one can make infinite regressions towards yet more symbolical significance without actually pausing to say that there may be good 'objective' reasons why people may prefer to live in the suburbs or New Towns rather than the Inner City. These reasons may be quite unconnected with ownership, control, anxiety, orderliness, snobbery or status aspirations.

In other words, Ruth Glass may be on the wrong tack in her emphasis on English snobbery as an explanation for English anti-urbanism. After all, newer buildings are generally less damp than older ones and are larger and more suitable for modern appliances. It is highly likely that people *prefer* dry walls and labour-saving devices, not because they symbolize anything else, but because it is better not to be cold or oppressed by drudgery. As David Lockwood has said: 'a washing machine is a washing machine is a washing machine'. In the same way, a modern house is a modern house is a modern house. Since most 'modern' houses—i.e. those less than sixty years old—have been built on the edges of cities and are usually in areas still regarded as suburbs, then collections of modern houses exist coincidentally in the 'suburbs'. There are other aspects of suburban life which should be regarded as good things—in themselves, rather than symbols of something else. We have already mentioned easy access to the countryside, and there are others, such as relative freedom from air and noise pollution, adequate playspace, newer and better schools, the sight of trees. Moreover, for many newly forming households, suburbia is the only location where they can find homes at a price they can afford. In almost all cities there is a rent or price pyramid: prices are highest and offer least good value near the centre, while they gradually decrease further and further beyond the Inner City ring. The combination of very long journeys to work and decent housing at prices they can afford is not necessarily a satisfactory situation for the young worker who may, in fact, hardly ever see his or her family. Indeed, it is arguable that part of the success of New Towns for those who settle in them is that they combine decent, good-value housing and easy access to nearby employment.

It seems absurd, therefore, to claim that suburbs represent certain things beyond what they have to offer in themselves. Obviously the suburbs are a combination of desirable good things, among which are space *and* higher status. Indeed, it could be said that the higher status and other symbols arise simply because many of the good things the suburb has to offer—for example, less air and noise pollution than in the Inner City—are in very short supply and that only those with access to adequate resources can get access to these good things, on anything approaching their own terms.

Again, this argument has important implications for those who

wish to move to New or Expanding Towns. Just as it seems
absurd to state that suburbanites are *only* seeking symbols of a
particular way of life, so it seems even more ridiculous to claim
the same for Inner City dwellers who wish to move to a New
or Expanding Town. For such households are likely to suffer
more from the relative disadvantages of the Inner City, in terms
of interference and disturbance, than those Inner City dwellers
who can eventually afford to buy a semi in the suburbs. This
is because in the City it is the poorest who bear the greatest
social costs of large-scale urbanization and these are the groups
least able to afford to buy themselves out either now or in the
future. For them the New or Expanding Town is the main realistic
means of gaining access to all the good things that the suburbs
have to offer. These good things include both the modern house
and the higher status. Thus, just as it is not possible to explain
exhaustively all moves to the suburbs in terms of status seeking
and a search for orderliness, so it is even less possible to explain
all moves to a New or Expanding Town in these terms.

Conclusions

It is time, briefly, to draw together the threads from these two
opening chapters, which have been concerned with the issue of
choice about where to live.

In the first chapter, we looked at the cohesiveness of the Inner
City community, and the values of those who have been living
there. Our conclusion was, first, that the pull of 'community'
may well have been exaggerated in the past; and this concept
looks particularly odd given that, second, it is generally accepted
that the working class is not homogeneous in terms of values.
If we accept the rough/respectable dichotomy there is probably
an important distinction to be made between those who aspire
to become more 'respectable' and those who consider themselves
respectable already but are worried in case their environment
becomes less so. In this way, we suggest there are 'respectable'
status aspirers and 'respectable' status maintainers. The former
will wish to move away from an area they consider is low-status
to one with higher status, whether the area of origin is changing
downwards in their estimation or not; the latter will wish to
move away *only if* they perceive their area of origin as changing

for the worse. In that chapter we also considered the different ways, deriving from the urban managerialist thesis and its developments, in which New Towns policy could be analysed.

In the second chapter, we considered the possible implications of various factors for movement out of the City—and out of London in particular. For example, those people who are concerned with obtaining or preserving their own status are likely to wish to move out. If they move to the suburbs, they can find a stable, and relatively homogeneous environment; they can also obtain (given that they can afford it) the benefits attached to owner-occupation: both tangible, in terms of better housing conditions, and intangible, in terms of status.

But the suburbs are also a good in themselves, providing for a better and in some senses freer way of life than the cities for particular kinds of household, and although those who move to a New or Expanding Town, as part of the planned migration process, will not usually also obtain their own house, as part of that process, they will nevertheless also enjoy these general benefits. In this sense, neither suburbanites nor people who wish to move to New Towns are merely status seekers: they are also seeking a rather easier, less stressful way of life.

These are the themes that we will use in trying to explain the data we have collected about people moving from Islington to New and Expanding Towns. But while these themes tell us about the complex of attitudes that we might expect to find among them and among the officials who operate the scheme for planned migration, they tell us little about which objective characteristics—in terms of age, income, colour, occupation— we might find among migrants to New or Expanding Towns. Previous migration studies, however, give us clues as to the objective characteristics of potential and actual migrants and it is to these we turn now.

References

1. HOWARD, EBENEZER, *Garden Cities of Tomorrow* (Faber, repr. 1965), p. 145.
2. ibid., pp. 155–6.
3. WARD, C., 'The Missing Half', *Town and Country Planning*, Vol. 41, No. 1, January 1973.
4. HOWARD, op. cit., p. 159.

5. OSBORN, F. J. and WHITTICK, ARNOLD, *The New Towns, answer to megalopolis* (Leonard Hill, 1969), p. 34.

6. JACOBS, JANE, *The Death and Life of Great American Cities* (Penguin, 1965), pp. 28–9.

7. Quoted in OSBORN and WHITTICK, op. cit., p. 21.

8. London County Council, *Housing of the Working Classes in London* (LCC, 1913).

9. In JACKSON, ALAN A., *Semi-Detached London* (George Allen and Unwin, 1973), p. 319.

10. ibid., esp. Chs. 8, 14–15.

11. Quoted in JACKSON, op. cit., p. 169.

12. PAHL, R. E., *Urbs in Rure: The Metropolitan Fringe in Hertfordshire* (LSE Geographical Papers, No. 2, 1965).

13. STEDMAN-JONES, G., *Outcast London* (Clarendon Press, 1971).

14. GLASS, RUTH, 'Anti-urbanism', quoted in STEWART, MURRAY, *The City* (Penguin Books, 1972).

15. DYOS, H. J., *Urbanity and Suburbanity* (Leicester University Press, 1973).

16. GLASS, RUTH, op. cit.

17. THOMAS, RAY, *London's New Towns* (PEP Broadsheet No. 510, April 1969), p. 377.

18. SIR FREDERIC OSBORN's preface to HOWARD's *Garden Cities of Tomorrow*, op. cit., p. 18.

19. Ministry of Town and Country Planning, *Interim Reports of the New Towns Committee* (Cmd 6759, HMSO, 1946).

20. Ministry of Town and Country Planning, *Final Reports of the New Towns Committee* (Cmd 6876, HMSO, 1946); para. 22.

21. LEWIS SILKIN in *Town and Country Planning*, Vol. 36, No. 1/2, Jan.–Feb. 1968, p. 18.

22. WYNDHAM THOMAS in Evans, H. (ed.), *New Towns: the British Experience* (Charles Knight, 1972), p. 46.

23. CARTER, EDWARD, *The Future of London* (Penguin Books, 1962), p. 57.

24. SCHAFFER, FRANK, *The New Town Story* (Paladin Books, 1972), p. 247.

25. THORNS, DAVID, *Suburbia* (Paladin Books, 1973), p. 18.

26. CLAWSON, M. and HALL, P., *Planning and Urban Growth: an Anglo-American Expansion* (Johns Hopkins University Press, 1973), p. 207.

Chapter Three

The Context for Migration

In the previous chapters we speculated about the kinds of attitudes that working-class people might have towards Inner City areas and New and Expanding Towns and how these attitudes might colour and determine their attitudes to moving from one area to the other. In this chapter we will look specifically at moving. This involves examining theories of migration—many of which would claim to tell us what kinds of people are more likely to move than others in terms of their 'objective' characteristics—e.g. their age, sex, marital status, socio-economic group, colour, level of occupational skill. Thus the discussion in this chapter should act as a counter-weight to the discussion of attitudes in the previous chapter.

It would be wrong to imply, however, that migration theories have nothing to say about the attitudes of migrants or potential migrants—they do, but many of these attitudes are linked by inference to so-called 'objective' characteristics. Thus migration theory encourages one to make statements like: 'Young people are more likely to move because they are at the family-building stage/more adventurous/more able to get mortgages,' or 'People threatened with redundancy unless they move are more likely to move for fear of losing their jobs.' In each case, attitudes to moving are ascribed to a particular 'objective' or actually determined state—e.g. being young or potentially unemployed. Thus it is impossible to divorce 'objective' characteristics from the attitudes accruing to them but what we can do is to use a combination of objective characteristics and attitudes drawn from our knowledge of migration theory to form hypotheses about who might move to New or Expanding Towns —in terms of their 'objective characteristics'.

Another important element in migration theory is the attention paid to the obstacles that prevent people from moving. Such obstacles might be highly personal to the potential migrant (e.g. fear of strange environments) thus preventing him or her from taking the initial steps towards movement, or they might be obstacles thrown up en route by institutions that prevent even extremely determined migrants from getting any further. Migration theories take account of both these kinds of constraint— which for shorthand purposes we can term 'personal' and 'public'. In the second half of this chapter we shall discuss the specifically 'public' opportunities and obstacles provided by the institutions that line the migrant's route to the New or Expanding Towns.

An early writer—Dorothy S. Thomas [1]—claimed in 1938, after looking at migration evidence spread over a long period of time and placed in several contexts, that 'there was only one consistent differential: age. People in their late teens, twenties or early thirties were more likely to move than other age groups.' But while this coincides with the evidence presented elsewhere in this book, it is unclear whether age can in any sense be described as an independent variable. For example, young people are usually at the beginning of jobs and independent family life. Marriage, which is very frequently said by migrants to be one of their main reasons for moving, occurs almost always between the late teens and the early thirties. Young heads of household are more likely to have rapidly expanding families and therefore need increasing amounts of space, and those that can, will move to larger dwellings.

Moreover, the fact of being young may emphasize attitudes that encourage people, of whatever age, to move. For example, young people may simply be more hopeful than older people. And, being young, this more adventurous spirit will be reinforced by their objective circumstances: they may not yet have put down the neighbourhood roots, made the friends, acquired the mortgage, begun educating the children which, as was suggested in Chapter 1, can be strong disincentives to move. They can afford to take greater risks because they themselves have less to lose, and the impact of their loss need not affect other members of their family, either because they have none, or because the family consists of people of a similar or very young age.

Another reason why young people are more likely to move is that they have greater command over the resources necessary to allow for a voluntary move. For example, Building Societies are more willing to lend to them, and, for skilled and professional young people, their more recent education may expand their job opportunities relative to other workers in an increasingly specialized world.

Thus we can legitimately assume that the movers to New or Expanding Towns are likely to be younger than the rest of the population. But we must bear in mind that such a fact, once it is established, tells us nothing about the underlying factors that cause or allow young people to move from one area to another.

Somewhat similar statements can be made about the often repeated result from migration studies — that skilled workers are more likely to move than unskilled. The implication usually is that the skilled are more aspirant—if middle-class they can be called 'career spiralists' and if working-class they can be called 'respectable' or 'imitative'. Clearly, in themselves, these statements are gross over-simplifications, since they fail to take account of the real differentiation of opportunities for people on particular career spirals or with particular skills. For people with highly specialized skills—e.g. doctors, university lecturers, high-level managers—the prospects of promotion within one labour market usually shrink as they move up the scale. Thus 'career spiralists' have to move in order to carry on spiralling. The situation is slightly different for skilled manual workers. While some skills are obviously highly area-specific—mining, for example—many are not; rather than force a man or woman to move on, it can be argued that a manual skill *allows* a person to move—if he or she wants to. Thus if a skilled worker wishes to improve his or her housing, but can only do so by moving from one labour market to another, then he or she will have greater opportunity to do so than his or her unskilled fellows. Thus occupational skill brings with it 'a series of constraints and opportunities which one can expect to combine to determine a high rate of movement.

Other commentators have suggested other 'objective' characteristics such as household type or stage in the life cycle. These and the factors mentioned above have been singled out in migration studies (Leslie and Richardson [2], Donnison [3],

Taylor [4], and Rossi [5]) and shown to be significant in many situations. However, Simmie [6] suggests that these kinds of study

> tend to over emphasise particular aspects of movement. One says that housing is the main reason for moving, another adds social and employment motives, others the connection between social and geographic mobility and education and others, again, show the connections between choice and the values derived from social class position.

He introduces a scheme which not only uses social class as the chief variable, but also uses it as an explanation for different motives for moving and different perceptions of obstacles to moving.

> The theory advanced here is that geographic mobility is the result of the interaction between the independent social structural variables of age and household structure within specific social classes and a set of intervening variables represented by a family's values and aspirations which lead it to seek net gains in the balance of satisfaction derived from housing, employment, location and social intercourse.

For example, he suggests that the shortage of housing and, hence, the relatively low quality of housing occupied by low-income groups will mean that the lower the social class the more likely people are to move primarily to better their *housing*. And because housing is in short supply, it will be given a relatively high value compared to other good things, such as environmental services, valued by other classes. Thus in studies such as this one, which concentrate on the movement of low social classes or socioeconomic groups, one would expect, if Simmie is right, particular kinds of motivation to move. One might infer, for example, that working-class households which consider themselves adequately housed will not wish to move, while those which think themselves badly housed might be very highly motivated indeed— while they are unlikely to be 'status aspirants'.

Simmie also argues that restricted movement leads to stronger kinship and friendship networks in small areas and it is likely that the lower the social class the stronger the desire to maintain these good contacts and, hence, there will be a greater reluctance to move long distances. Empirical data from Amelia Harris' *Labour Mobility in Great Britain* [7] tend to confirm this contention. She showed that for moves up to 10 miles, 68 per cent of the movers gave housing reasons for moving, compared with 8.5 per cent giving work reasons. On the other hand, for moves of distances between 31 and 100 miles, 46.0 per cent of movers gave work reasons for moving. Given that New and Expanding Towns tend to be at least 31 miles away from the migrants' areas of origin, then one would expect those moving there to be atypical in one or all of the following ways: they perceive their housing need as so pressing that they are prepared to move very long distances in order to better it, or they have less good kinship and friendship networks concentrated in their areas of origin, or they have kinship and friendship networks but they no longer regard them as particularly important. Data from the National Movers' Survey conducted by the Office of Population Census and Surveys (OPCS) and covering the year October 1970 to October 1971 broadly confirm this picture. They show that moves *within* London tend to be overwhelmingly on the grounds of housing (cited by 55 per cent of respondents) as opposed to jobs (cited by only 4 per cent). Moves *out* of London follow the same pattern, but less emphatically— 48 per cent give housing as the reason, and 19 per cent jobs. But, finally, the pattern reverses itself altogether for moves *into* London—only 17 per cent give housing as the reason, as opposed to 56 per cent giving jobs. In either of the latter cases, long-distance moves for working-class people need not be as problematic as Simmie implies.

An alternative perspective is suggested by Michael Mann's *Workers on the Move* [8]. He found that high proportions of manual workers were prepared to move nearly fifty miles in order to keep their jobs: only a few moved for housing reasons. He uses the concept of *economic dependence* to show that workers will seek security and stability from a firm in which they have worked for a fair length of time and in which they have learnt to have confidence in a liberal and generous management. In this case, rather than risk job insecurity, the workers moved in very large numbers from Birmingham to Banbury. Thus one might expect that some migrants move to New or Expanding Towns not primarily to better their housing but rather to keep their jobs. These would be the workers employed by firms that

make the decision to move and wish to take their workers with
them and close down the plant, warehouse, store in the area
of origin.

The migration studies mentioned above suggest at least five
characteristics the migrants studied here might have: they might
be young, they might be highly skilled, they might move
because they are threatened with redundancy, they might be
moving largely for housing reasons since they are a working-class
population, and they might be 'exceptional' because they move
long distances. But such studies tell us nothing about whether
migrants have such characteristics because people 'like this' are
particularly highly motivated or have better opportunities to
move than others. In order to begin to assess how far opportunities and their constraints will determine who moves to New
or Expanding Towns it is now necessary to look at the procedures
that process planned migration. From this analysis will emerge
a clearer picture of the objective characteristics—in terms of age,
occupational skills—of those who have moved in the past and
some explanations as to why those patterns of movement exist.
The following sections refer to the selection system in London
only.

Opportunities for Londoners to move to New or Expanding Towns

There are a number of different ways in which Londoners can
move to a New or Expanding Town. Some are common to either
destination: for example, an individual head of household can
register on what is now called the New and Expanding Towns
Scheme (NETS)—formerly the Industrial Selection Scheme.
Alternatively, a firm moving to a New or Expanding Town
may offer all or some of its present employees the opportunity
to move with it. Other opportunities are specific to a particular
move: for example, a chance to move to a New Town may arise
as a result of particular linking arrangements made between a
London Borough and a specific New Town. Or an individual
may move to a particular town entirely on his own initiative.
This last example underlines another distinction: in some
instances each person involved in the move has to play an
active role in bringing it about; in others—for example, the

case of a 'migrant' firm—individuals can be completely passive in the opportunity-creating process and simply have to make a decision whether to grasp a given opportunity or not. The following paragraphs attempt to explain how these procedures constrain, and in some senses determine what kind of people make the move.

The Industrial Selection Scheme[1]

In the words of the Greater London Development Plan, the Industrial Selection Scheme

> ... devised in 1953, is a list of persons who wish to move to an Expanding or New Town. The object of the scheme is to ensure that when finding houses and jobs for Londoners in Expanding and New Towns priority shall, *so far as is consistent with the demands of industry*, be given to those in housing need, or to moves which result in the indirect relief of housing need, e.g. the movement of a Council tenant releases a dwelling in London which can be used for an urgent housing case.

Thus, the Scheme is an attempt to reconcile two primary objectives; that of relieving housing need (as defined by the GLC) in London, and that of providing for the labour demands of employers in New and Expanding Towns which have an arrangement to take overspill population from London. To this end, those who register on the ISS with the GLC for housing in New and Expanding Towns must satisfy two main requirements: they must be resident in the Greater London area or be tenants of the GLC outside that area, and also be willing to take up employment in the town. (Provision is also made for servicemen, recently discharged, who were formerly domiciled in London; workers who move with their firms out of London; and pensioners with relatives in a New or Expanding Town.)

The scheme, as an administrative procedure, is managed by the GLC (called the 'exporting authority') and the Department

---

[1] This section is based on work done for the research project by Charles Thomson. His work has been published elsewhere; see Charles Thomson: *The Industrial Selection Scheme—a study of conflicting objectives in urban and regional planning.* (Centre for Environmental Studies, 1973).

of Employment, but also involves the Department of the Environment, and the New and Expanding Towns themselves (called the 'receiving authorities'). An intending migrant first applies, either directly or through his or her borough Housing Department, to the GLC for registration in the GLC's Industrial Selection Scheme. The GLC Housing Department having checked on the applicant's eligibility (as indicated in the previous paragraph) and on his or her degree of 'housing need', then sends his or her application card to the Department of Employment for occupational classification. All necessary information about the applicant is now held by the GLC and Department of Employment.

Meanwhile, the employer in the New or Expanding Town notifies his or her local employment exchange of the vacancies he or she has to offer, is asked to fill as many as he or she can locally, after which any unfilled vacancies (notified under 'orders') are notified to the Department's London and South-East Regional Office, and thence to the GLC and to all sixty employment exchanges in the Greater London area. The GLC then sends details of up to twenty suitably qualified applicants to the Regional Office, whereupon the Department of Employment notifies suitable applicants of the vacancies and, in the majority of cases, submits those who are willing for interview to the employer. Applicants may then be engaged by the employer in the New or Expanding Town. As far as employment is concerned, then, the mesh through which potential migrants have to move is a tight one. First, an employer has to offer a job to his or her local employment exchange, which means that some jobs will be filled locally—particularly the unskilled ones. Secondly, the GLC has to pick out 'suitable' applicants in terms of occupational skill and 'housing need' and from thence the employer will select out the applicants he or she thinks best.

It is therefore clear that the prime determinant of the sorts of people who move to New or Expanding Towns is the type of *jobs* that are available in those towns; also that it is the employers who, within broad limits, control migration to those towns. The effect of employment demands dominating migration to New or Expanding Towns will become clearer when we look at the occupational skill levels of actual migrants.

But the way in which those who operate the scheme choose

to define priorities, in terms of housing need, is almost equally important. Here, the key question is how 'housing need' is defined and acted upon. In this case, it is not simply a question of measuring 'housing need' along a chosen scale and then giving those in most need priority. While all households except owner-occupiers are classified into four categories of need, the definition of which is based on a combined index of a lack of standard facilities and overcrowding, it does not necessarily follow that householders in the top category will get priority. In fact tenants of the GLC, London Borough Councils, and Housing Associations, who are assumed to be in satisfactory housing, are given priority on the basis of the assumption that their movement to New or Expanding Towns creates vacancies in London for those in 'housing need'. This procedure is based on the assumption that, as a Support Paper prepared by the GLC for the Greater London Development Plan Inquiry claimed: 'the movement of a council tenant releases a dwelling in London which can be used for an urgent housing case'. In addition, those who are registered on a local authority waiting list receive priority over those not so registered, on the grounds that movement of the former to a New or Expanding Town reduces the length of the waiting lists and thus the size of the obligations of local authorities to rehouse. Thus the effect of the way in which the mesh in the Housing Department operates is very far from ensuring that those defined as being in the greatest 'housing need' are given the greatest opportunity to move. There are numerous diversions en route, and those diversions may well, in effect, favour council tenants already adequately housed.

The Department of Employment's side of the operation is concerned with the assessment of the employment skills of those who have registered on the Scheme, and with the submission of suitable applicants for interview with employers who are unable to fill all their vacancies locally. Thus a system of occupational classification has been devised in order to describe employment skills adequately for the purpose of submission to employers. In addition, a system called 'staging' of occupations is used by the Department of Employment to indicate degree of shortage. The purpose of this system is to provide for certain administrative 'short-cuts' in the case of occupations for which demand is great and supply small, to ensure the speedy submission of suitable applicants to employers. Other things being equal, those who are council tenants and those on the waiting lists with a high degree of 'housing need' will always be given preference over other applicants, but the choice of the employer ultimately determines who is selected. We are, after all, talking about an *industrial* selection scheme. The contradictions between this outcome and the original objectives of planned migration, set out at length in Chapter 2, will immediately be apparent.

For the Scheme is not a 'social service', designed simply to help those with housing problems to move to better circumstances elsewhere, but rather an administrative device aimed at reducing the burden of the rehousing obligations of local authorities at the same time as providing for the labour requirements of employers. This point is further illustrated by the fact that, as Sheila Ruddy has shown, the scope of the list has been progressively widened since it was started in 1953, beyond those in 'housing need' and those linked by borough of residence to specific New Towns, to include *any* Londoner wanting to move to *any* New or Expanding Town. This widening was effected simply to get more people moved and therefore widen the scale of the Scheme, so that the demands of industry were reckoned as being at least as significant as the wishes of London boroughs to lighten the burden of their housing programmes.

But another result has been that the Scheme has tended to discriminate in another way which is of importance for our general theme, in terms of the areas within London from which it draws.

After the coming into being of the new London government structure in 1965 the catchment area for the Industrial Selection Scheme operations was enlarged from the old administrative county to include the entire Greater London area and all resident households became eligible for rehousing through the scheme. Up to April 1965, the LCC had housed 15 000 families in overspill communities.

The formation of the GLC led to a notable expansion of the overspill programme. Between 1962–6, 79 per cent of families moving through the ISS were from the sectoral equivalent of the inner boroughs and the annual outflow was estimated at 2500 a year. Between 1967–72 only 56 per cent of the outflow was from inner London, but this had risen (numerically) to 3500 families a year. Obviously the enlargement of the 'statutory exporting area' for the London ISS has been of particular advantage to the outer suburbs—particularly those in the outer North-West where industrial movement to expanding towns in the western sector[2] of the Outer Metropolitan Area has been particularly important [9]. About 12 per cent of all moves are with transferring firms.

Table 3 I

Characteristics of sample GLC families only

	1962–6	1967–72	1962–72
Transferred workers	19%	12%	15%
Borough tenants	3%	11%	7%
LCC—GLC tenants	6%	8%	7%
All tenants	9%	19%	14%
Inner London			
% all moves	79	56	66
% transferred workers	66	31	51
Outer London			
% all moves	21	44	34
% transferred workers	34	69	49

Source: Sample Survey of GLC records, 1972

Sample Base	670	869	1539

One of the important results of the pattern of dispersal fostered by the GLC is that the outer boroughs actually gain from County Hall a good deal more than they give in housing terms. For every three dwellings provided for inhabitants of the outer suburbs by County Hall, the Boroughs give back through the Nomination Scheme only one—a substantial subsidy to the affluent suburbs at the expense of the Inner City. Even if the total pool system (see Chapter 4) is brought into the equation, there are still as many families leaving outer London through the ISS as are moving in from inner London through the pool system; roughly 2300 each year.

The ISS is basically a system for channelling London families

---

[2] Prior to 1965 only certain towns—Swindon, Bletchley—accepted Londoners from the suburbs.

to Expanding Towns, but the New Towns, too, appear to favour outer London. Roderick [10] has shown that of the 64 000 households who moved from Greater London to the New Towns between 1961–4, 60 per cent originated from outer boroughs. Between 1961–6, of the annual outflow of 40 000 migrants from Inner London to the South-East region, about 3000 went to New Towns (8 per cent). As Heraud has argued [11], the fact that the chief beneficiaries have been Harrow, Barnet, Enfield, Redbridge, Newham and Barking, shows that the parts of London with least housing stress benefit disproportionately from the New Towns policy.

It is in these ways that the notions of employers in New and Expanding Towns concerning the reliability and contributions to profitability of potential employees, and of Housing Managers concerning cleanliness and financial stability of potential tenants combine to ensure that screening of applicants through the Scheme especially favours the 'respectable working class'—that is, skilled manual workers.

Having seen that the type of firm that becomes involved with a New or Expanding Town is a crucial determinant of who moves, we turn to the second set of organizational devices designed to promote and control the movement of industry to New or Expanding Towns.

Movement of industry from London

For a long period after the Second World War, the London County Council had among its principal objectives the encouragement of decentralization from the metropolis. This goal was inherited by the Greater London Council, as its successor, and held good up to, and including the preparation of the original version of the Greater London Development Plan, which repeated the Council's commitment to encourage factories and offices which can operate equally effectively elsewhere to move to New or Expanding Towns (or to the GLC's own development at Thamesmead, in appropriate cases) by voluntary negotiation [12]. In New Towns, co-operation with the Development Corporations is essential; and in the case of Expanding Towns, the GLC itself has pursued this objective under the Town Development agreements negotiated with the individual Expanding Towns. In both cases, the aim is not only to match the housing and employment needs of people who move to these places, but also to create a self-contained community [13]. The GLC and the Department of Environment have shared the executive duty of making decentralization of employment to New and Expanding Towns work successfully. Each has, therefore, sponsored a permanent advisory service through which potential migrant firms or offices can obtain information, namely the Industrial Centre[3] and the Location of Offices Bureau, respectively.

It is only comparatively recently that the implications of continued loss of population and employment for London have led the GLC to conduct a fundamental reappraisal of its policy. We consider this reappraisal in greater detail in a later chapter; for present purposes, we will continue to explore the broad principles of policy on planned migration, as they still held good in 1972, when the bulk of the work on the study was undertaken. One determinant in the implementation of this policy by the various agencies involved has been the structure of regional policy and the system of incentives and constraints set up under it: another is the general economic climate within which the policy has to operate. The first is also explored at greater length in a later chapter: in this section, we will consider the relative significance of the economic climate (including rate of growth and expansion) and the changing structure of industry, technology and labour demand, and other constraints on movement.[4]

The period covered by our investigation (1970–2) was one of economic recession, which was bound to affect significantly the volume and quality of the movement of industry and employment. The slow economic growth that characterized this period was both cause and effect of limited expansion. Where demand was not sufficiently elastic, expansion was considered unprofitable and was, therefore, limited. In spite of this general tendency, movement continued to take place during this period, but on a limited scale. Rates of growth varied considerably between and within industries, at periods of stagnation just as they do during periods of economic boom. Consequently, even

---

[3] Now (1976) known as the London Industrial Centre, with somewhat different functions.

[4] The section that follows is based mainly on work done by Ukwu Ejionye as part of the original research project.

during this period firms within the growth areas of industries continued to move: service industries, engineering, electrical and scientific instruments, metal goods and metal castings; paper, printing and publishing; motor vehicles and aircraft; chemicals; food; drinks and tobacco [14].

The essential point about these areas of continued expansion is that they highlight the changing structure of industry in general: the continuing contraction of the extractive industries, slower expansion of the manufacturing industries and rapid expansion of service industries. The service sector is heavily concentrated in the South-East Region, while manufacturing is increasingly becoming capital-intensive [15]. This structural change can be explained in part by increasing technological innovation and the need to improve the efficiency of labour. At the same time, the emphasis on economic rationalization—efficiency, competitiveness, cost reduction and profit maximization—supplies the justification (in economic terms) for the use of capital-intensive plants at new locations.

The net effects of all these factors (the economic climate, the changing structure of industry and technological innovations) have been disappointing, if success is measured in terms of the volume of movement and the generation of employment suitable for different types of labour moving out of London. Capital-intensive plants create fewer jobs; and the employment structure is increasingly weighted in favour of the skilled and those with professional qualifications; the economic recession severely limits expansion and the volume of industrial movement, even if allowance is made for rapid growth in certain areas. In this kind of situation, migration must inevitably be highly selective, both in terms of employment generated and the type of labour currently required by employers.

Within the context of these general determinants of industrial movement, the Government operates a controlling device which basically consists of a permission to move. By the Town and Country Planning Act of 1947, the Board of Trade was given the power to regulate the establishment of new industrial undertakings or the extension of existing ones, through the issue or refusal of Industrial Development Certificates (IDCs). This power extends only to factories; and until 1976, it excluded those of less than 5000 square feet in Greater London, and extensions of less than 10 per cent of existing space. Unless the firm is too small to require a certificate, or is specifically exempted from this requirement (as in the case of a warehouse), failure to obtain a Certificate may prevent a firm from carrying out a planned move. A parallel system of control has been operated over office employment since 1964. Office Development Permits (ODPs) are required before developers can apply for planning permission; since 1970 this form of control has only operated in London and the South-East. The level at which it operated was originally set at 3000 square feet; in 1967, it was raised to 10 000, and in 1976 to 15 000 square feet.

A Department of Trade and Industry survey [16] shows that the refusal or expected refusal of an Industrial Development Certificate influenced initial thinking about a move in 12 per cent of the cases studied. Refusal was an outstanding single cause in 9 per cent of the cases classified as 'labour-intensive industries'. In the present study, three of four firms investigated indicated that it was not easy for them to obtain Certificates. Getting one involved a long period of protracted argument, meetings and consultations with the government departments responsible. In planning a move, timing is an essential element. Delay in obtaining an IDC is not only frustrating but can cause the loss of valuable opportunities.

But in assessing the effects of these delays one must also recognize the problems that the Department of Industry faces in processing an application for a Certificate. Their task is the effective exercise of the discretion conferred by the Distribution of Industries Act 1945, by directing and controlling the location of industries in such a way as to achieve a balance between population and employment, and between the regions, in terms of industrial development. However, the exact operation of these rules has been obscure; and critics have argued that there should be more permanent procedural rules which would be comprehensive and available to the public, on the basis of which applications for Industrial Development Certificates could be processed. Some of these problems were recognized in the 1972 White Paper on regional policy [17]. This White Paper accepted the need to relax the rules relating to the granting of IDCs and coupled this with further financial incentives designed to encourage industrial mobility. Subsequently, the accumulation of evidence that the economic situation in London was deteriorating led to some specific concessions being made, both on industrial and on office employment. On IDCs, the Government announced in March 1976 that in future Certificates could be issued for the speculative redevelopment of old industrial sites in order to provide some help in dealing with the problem of industrial obsolescence in London. In the following month the exemption limit for Certificates was raised to 12 500 square feet in the South-East and the Minister of Planning and Local Government, in announcing a similar relaxation for ODPs, indicated that in the light of changed circumstances he was prepared to reconsider the role of the Location of Offices Bureau. However, at the time of writing it is too early to say what the effect of these changes will be.

Once a firm has made the decision to move and been granted permission, other factors come into play that affect the kinds of staff they will take with them. One factor of the utmost importance to migrant firms is the retention of existing staff and the availability of labour at the new location [18]. Expansion implies a need for more labour, especially the skilled, technicians, specialists and professional staff. There has been for some time a shortage in these categories of labour throughout the South-East Region [19], and firms therefore try to ensure that they retain at least their key workers. In fact, firms often depend on these key workers to help make their choice of location and to continue operations during the transitional period. As a result, firms must prepare themselves for heavy additional expenditure in order to retain existing labour (and key workers in particular): this may involve offering higher salaries and higher fringe benefits; paying generous grants to cover moving costs, family and disturbance allowances; and giving financial assistance towards house purchase and soft furnishings. There were cases reported of firms 'pinching' workers from others, and some firms having to close down after a move as a result of labour shortage. At the other extreme, it is also alleged that a move can serve as an opportunity for a firm to rid itself of its undesirable or inefficient labour through redundancy or retirement, or by failure to provide the necessary incentive to move. Such labour problems have forced potential migrant firms to give very careful consideration to the distance of the move and the direction of movement. Studies conducted for the *Strategic Plan for the South-East* showed that the further away from London a firm moves, the less of its existing staff it is able to retain. On average, firms recruited 57 per cent of their labour at the new site, a proportion which varied significantly with the distance of the move; firms which moved over forty miles tended to recruit most of their labour at the new site [20]. A significant relationship was also found between availability of labour and the size of population at the new location. Larger centres of employment with a variety of different types of firms are more likely to provide a wide range of opportunities than small centres where opportunities will be limited to relatively few firms. This was the basic reason for difficulty experienced by firms located in small centres (measured by their population) in the recruitment of labour, and it also provides a partial explanation for firms' choice of location in the more populated parts of the South-East region.

To sum up, there is a complex of factors, all of which mean that it is considerably easier for a potential migrant with skills to move to a New or Expanding Town than it is for an unskilled potential migrant. Among these is the fact that the type of firm that moves is usually capital-intensive and an employer of relatively skilled labour, and that firms that move will attempt to keep their skilled labour and can be confident they can recruit unskilled labour from the hinterland. At the same time, although the New or Expanding Towns are in theory intended to counterbalance this emphasis on employment demand by taking account of housing 'need', the actual operation of that definition in practice gives priority to those already adequately housed—i.e. council tenants, many of whom will, anyway, be skilled workers.

The Composition of Movement to New and Expanding Towns

Before concluding this chapter, let us look at some of the data available about the objective characteristics of migrants to New and Expanding Towns from London. Have they, as we would now expect, been particularly young and particularly skilled? Table 3 II shows the age of migrants from Greater London to New and Expanding Towns in 1966—still, ten years later, the latest date for which full information was available. It is clear from the table that approximately two-thirds of the migrants were part of young families—either as parents or children—

since over one-third were in the age group 25 to 44, and just under one-third were children aged 14 and under.

Table 3 II

Age structure of population movement from Greater London to New and Expanding Towns 1966

| | Planned population movement from Greater London to public housing in New and Expanding Towns (1966) | |
	London New Towns*	Expanding Towns†
Age	%	%
1–14	28	32
15–19	4	5
20–24	16	16
25–44	35	34
45–RA‡	10	10
RA+	7	3
Total	100	100

Source: 1966 Census.

* Basildon, Bracknell, Crawley, Harlow, Hatfield, Hemel Hempstead, Stevenage, Welwyn Garden City.

† Andover, Ashford, Aylesbury, Banbury, Basingstoke, Bletchley, Bury St Edmunds, Haverhill, Huntingdon, King's Lynn, Letchworth, Luton, Mildenhall/Brandon, Peterborough, St Neots, Sudbury/Melford, Swindon, Thetford, Wellingborough, Witham.

‡ Retirement age, 60 for women and 65 for men; thus category RA+ signifies all men over 65 and women over 60.

While this evidence confirms that migrants are predominantly youthful, it tells us nothing about why this should be so—that is, whether the young are more likely to choose to move, or whether they are more likely to gain access to the resources and opportunities that are the necessary conditions of a move. Fortunately, we have data that can begin to fill out this picture. Using data on the age of heads of household collected for the survey of registrants on the Industrial Selection Scheme, and data collected by the GLC and the DE about GLC residents and migrants to six selected London New Towns, we can begin to assess the interplay between desire and opportunity as far as age is concerned. In column (i) of Table 3 III we have the age structure of heads of household registered on the ISS

—i.e. the ages of heads of household that so positively desired to move to a New or Expanding Town in 1971–2 that they had registered on the list of London residents wishing to move. Column (ii) shows the age structure of household heads who actually moved in 1969 to six selected towns and column (iii) shows the age structure of Greater London household heads in 1971, taken from unpublished census data—the years of the surveys quoted in the table do not completely coincide, but it is very unlikely that age structures for any of the three groups would vary markedly from one year to another. The table tells us a number of interesting things. First, heads of household registered on the ISS were considerably younger than heads of household living in the Greater London area as a whole. The most impressive differences are those at both ends of the age scale—very young heads of household (15–24) positively wanted to move out of all proportion to their numbers in the resident population—24 per cent of the former compared to 7 per cent of the latter. At the same time, hardly any very old people over 65 (0.2 per cent) wanted to move compared to the numbers

Table 3 III

Age of heads of households, ISS registrants*, migrants to six London New Towns†, GLC residents‡

Age	(i) ISS registrants (1971)	(ii) Married heads of household who moved to 6 London New Towns (1969)	(iii) Greater London residents (1971)
0–4	—		
5–14	—	—	—
15–24	23.7	24.4	6.7
25–34	34.7	34.4	15.1
35–44	17.9	17.4	15.9
45–54	13.5	11.4	36.7
55–64	10.0	5.9	
65+	0.2	6.6	26.5
Total	100	100	100

* This survey of registrants was carried out by Charles Thomson in 1971.

† These figures taken from statistics kindly lent by the Economic Directorate B Department of the Environment. The six new towns are Basildon, Bracknell, Crawley, Harlow, Hemel Hempstead and Stevenage.

‡ Unpublished census data kindly made available by the GLC Intelligence Unit.

in the Greater London population over retirement age (26.5 per cent). More than twice as many people in the 25–34 age group wanted to move as lived in the GLC area, but half as many in the 55–64 age group had registered on the ISS.

The picture seems clear; young people want to move to New or Expanding Towns, out of all proportion to their numbers in the Greater London population. But column (ii) gives us some indication of who succeeds in moving—in terms of age. Between the ages of 15 and 44 the proportion of household heads moving within each age band is very similar to the proportions registered on the ISS and, again, quite different from the GLC population. But the proportions of those moving compared to registrants on the ISS drop away between the ages of 45 and 64, only to rise again after the age of 65. Considerably more old people were moving in 1969 than one would expect from the proportions of elderly amongst ISS registrants—although still fewer than one might expect from the proportions of old in the Greater London population as a whole. This indicates that New and Expanding Towns recruit both the young and active and the old and inactive—but the middle-aged fare comparatively badly. This pattern probably reflects the priority that most Towns give to the retired parents of residents. The disproportionately high number of old people actually moving to New Towns, compared to the proportion registered on the Scheme, is a reflection of wider opportunities for this age group, although the comparatively small numbers of old people in Greater London who have registered on the scheme is a reflection of the relative lack of desire to move

In summary, this table reveals something both about motivation to move and about opportunities. It shows that the young are highly motivated and have proportionate access to New or Expanding towns, that the old are not highly motivated but have disproportionately high access, and that the middle-aged are not very highly motivated but many potential middle-aged movers must be disappointed.

A similar exercise with socio-economic groups will show the proportions of potential movers, actual movers, and GLC residents who fall into particular SEGs. These are presented in Table 3 IV. This shows up three major imbalances between the proportions of certain SEGs registered on the Scheme and the proportions in Greater London as a whole. There were proportionately more skilled manual workers, far fewer professional and managerial workers, and more than twice as many unskilled workers registered on the Scheme as there were living in the GLC area in 1971. This implies that desire to move to New or Expanding Towns is low among the higher social classes, higher among skilled manual workers and highest among unskilled workers. Column (ii) in Table 3 IV gives us some idea

Table 3 IV

Migrants to six London New and Expanding Towns*, ISS registrants, Greater London residents† by socio-economic group

SEG	(i) ISS registrants (1971)	(ii) Migrants to 8 New Towns (1971)	(iii) Greater London residents (1971)
Professional (3, 4)	0.8	7.1	6.1
Managerial (1, 2, 13)	3.0	10.8	13.9
Skilled manual (8, 9, 12, 14)	42.5	39.9	32.9
Non-manual, and personal service workers (5, 6)	17.1	20.5	23.5
Semi-skilled and agricultural (7, 10, 15)	16.8	15.5	13.4
Unskilled manual (11)	19.9	4.7	7.2
Armed Forces and others (16, 17)	—	1.6	3.2
Total	100	100	100

Eight New Towns as in Table 3 III.
Not all columns add up to 100, due to rounding up.

* See note 2 to Table 3 III for source.

† Columns (ii) and (iii) refer to economically active or retired males aged 15 and over.

about what proportions of these three groups actually got to eight London New Towns in 1971. If these figures are a fair reflection of what has been happening over a longer period (and by considering other years, we can confirm that it is) they show that considerably fewer unskilled workers moved to these New Towns than one would expect from the preceding discussion of migration theory—that the poor and badly housed wish to move, but are frustrated by the obstacles thrown in their way by the planned migration process, which inevitably recruits disproportionately few unskilled workers.

Conclusions

In this chapter we have isolated a number of probable objective characteristics of migrants, using both migration theory and what we know of the machinery for movement of people and industry to New and Expanding Towns. The data about two of the more important characteristics—age and occupational skill—help to unravel part of the interplay between motivation and opportunity. It is clear that young people (i.e. those under 44) are very keen to move and, on the whole, manage to do so. Older people, particularly the very old, are not so keen to move and those between the ages of 45 and 64 have restricted opportunities. However, the planned migration process does seem to widen opportunities for the retired who wish to move—in this single instance, that of the movement of old-age pensioners, it seems that planned migration has some 'bite'. When we looked at socio-economic groups we found a pattern very similar to the one we would expect, given general migration theory and our knowledge of the kinds of industry that move to New and Expanding Towns. Unskilled workers are highly restricted in opportunities whereas skilled workers move in the expected proportion.

References

1. THOMAS, DOROTHY S., 'Research Memorandum on Migration Differentials', *Social Science Research Council Bulletin*, 43, New York, 1938.

2. LESLIE, G. R. and RICHARDSON, A. H., 'Life Cycle Career and the Decision to Move', *American Sociological Review*, **26**, 1961, pp. 894–902.

3. DONNISON, D. V., *The Government of Housing* (Penguin, 1967).

4. TAYLOR, R. C., 'Migration and Motivation' in J. A. Jackson (ed.), *Migration* (Cambridge University Press, 1969).

5. ROSSI, R. H., *Why Families Move: a study in the social psychology of urban residential mobility* (Glencoe: Free Press, 1955).

6. SIMMIE, JAMES, *The Sociology of Internal Migration* (Centre for Environmental Studies, UWP 15, 1972).

7. HARRIS, AMELIA I. and CLAUSEN, ROSEMARY, *Labour Mobility in Great Britain, 1952–63* (HMSO, 1967).

8. MANN, MICHAEL, *Workers on the Move* (Cambridge University Press, 1973).

9. KEEBLE, D. E., 'Industrial migration from N.W. London 1940–64', *Urban Studies*, Vol. 2, No. 1, May 1965, pp. 15–32.

10. RODERICK, W., 'The London New Towns: origin of migrants up to Dec. 1968', *Town Planning Review*, Vol. 42, No. 4, October 1971, pp. 323–34.

11. HERAUD, B., 'The New Towns and London's Housing Problem', *Urban Studies*, Vol. 3, No. 1, February 1966, pp. 8–21.

12. Statement in Greater London Development Plan (Greater London Council, 1969).

13. Ministry of Town and Country Planning, *Interim Reports of the New Towns Committee*, op. cit.

14. HOWARD, R. S., *The Movement of Manufacturing Industries in the U.K., 1946–65* (HMSO, 1968); HOWARD, R. S., *Movement of Industry: its role and generation* (paper presented at Cambridge Conference on Industrial Movement, Sept. 1971).

South-East Joint Planning Team, *Strategic Plan for the South-East*: studies Vol. 1, Population and Employment (HMSO, 1971).

15. HOWARD's Cambridge conference paper, op. cit.

16. Department of Trade and Industry, *Industrial movement 1964–7* (1969).

17. Department of Trade and Industry, *Industrial and regional development* (Cmd 4942, HMSO, 1972).

18. South-East Joint Planning Team, *Strategic Plan for the South-East*: Studies Vol. 5, Report of Economic Consultants Ltd (HMSO, 1971).

19. HOWARD's Cambridge conference paper, op. cit.

20. *Strategic Plan for the South-East*: Studies Vol. 5, op. cit., pp. 9–10.

Chapter Four

Conditions and Opportunities in an Inner London Borough

Having considered in the first three chapters some of the general reasons why people might wish to move to a New or Expanding Town, we now turn to a particular situation in the London Borough of Islington. In choosing Islington for more detailed examination, we had two factors in mind. The main one was that Islington stands out among the Inner London boroughs as having a particularly bad housing shortage; the 1971 census shows that only one other London borough—Kensington and Chelsea—had a higher proportion of population living at more than one and a half persons per room. At the same time, Islington has a high proportion of unskilled workers, and the second lowest average household income in Greater London, after Hackney [1]. Thus, if we wanted to find groups most likely to be highly motivated to move to a New or Expanding Town because they were badly housed and at the same time least likely to get to one because they were unskilled workers, Islington seemed a part of London that would highlight both motivation and opportunity—or the lack of them. The second reason for selecting Islington was that it is affected, in greater or lesser measure, by almost all the pressing problems that afflict Inner London as a whole.

The Inner London Context

The problems of Inner London are, very broadly, of two kinds.

First, there is an increasing imbalance between the jobs that are available in the inner areas and the skills that their inhabitants possess; and, second, there is a substantial shortage of accessible housing of adequate standard, at a price that either existing inhabitants or newcomers to the city can afford. The loss of jobs has been particularly acute in the manufacturing sector, where London has lost a quarter of the available jobs in the decade between 1961 and 1971; and it has affected the inner areas particularly severely. At the same time, the rapid decline in the numbers of dwellings in the privately rented sector has steadily reduced the amount of cheaper, readily accessible housing in Inner London.

Nor has the increased level of provision of housing in the public sector succeeded in eliminating housing stress in terms of the sharing of dwellings and the density at which housing space is used. The stress areas defined by the GLC for the Greater London Development Plan, which are the 10 per cent of wards in the conurbation with the highest indices of sharing and overcrowding [2], form a continuous belt running from Hammersmith in the West to Hackney and Newham in the East encircling the central area. Apart from the sharing of dwellings and overcrowding, there is also substantial obsolescence of dwellings, since much of the housing stock was built before the outbreak of the First World War and, because of inadequate maintenance or sheer age, is reaching the end of its useful life.

The Islington Case

All these problems—and others that bear almost as heavily on the inhabitants of the inner areas—are present in Islington. In giving an account of them, we shall draw on data from the 1971 census (where it has been published) and our own 1971 survey, which was carried out in an area of particularly bad housing within the London Borough of Islington. These data will help us to understand what conditions in Islington were like—in terms of housing and social structure—in 1971, how they were changing and what kinds of people were moving in and out of the Borough. This in turn will help to explain why people were moving within and beyond Islington, and what opportunities there were for Islington residents to better their housing or move to a New or Expanding Town.

The Borough of Islington lies immediately north of the expanding office complex of the City and with ready access to the transport and wholesale activities of East London and the mainline railway termini. The prosperous middle-class enclaves of Canonbury and Highbury, where highly paid office workers employed in Central London have bought Georgian homes, contrast with the shabbier and more cosmopolitan wards where poorly paid ethnic minorities have settled, drawn to the low-skilled service jobs of the railways, the distributive services and some offices. These wards fall mostly in the northern part of the Borough, where a series of intensive investigations have been undertaken by the North Islington Housing Rights Group, with support from Shelter [3]. The Group's conclusions about housing circumstances in Upper Holloway—and in particular the problems of the large number of ill-equipped and badly maintained Victorian terraced houses—hold good for large tracts of North Islington. Somewhere between these extremes—geographically and in terms of circumstances—are the municipal estates, still, in 1971, inhabited mainly by the English-born working class.

One simple way of assessing the extent of the pressures that exist within the Islington housing market is to establish how far the existing stock of dwellings falls short of catering for the present population, at acceptable space standards. This method of striking a balance sheet has obvious drawbacks but gives a broad indication of the numerical level of deficiency. Measured in this way, the Borough Planning Officer estimated that in 1971 (when the present study was undertaken) there was a crude deficit of 17 000 dwellings in Islington; some 77 000 households were then living in 60 000 dwellings. This was an improvement on 1966 figures, when the crude deficit was nearer 27 000, but still implies that one household in five in the Borough is sharing accommodation [4]. This shortage has been exacerbated by the rapid increase that has taken place in the proportion of small households in the Inner London population. In absolute terms, the population of Inner London has been in decline since before the First World War; but the number of households has remained more stable. The effect of this phenomenon can be clearly observed, in the case of Islington, by making a comparison between the population of the Borough in 1961 and at the Censuses of 1966 and 1971. During that period, the total population of the Borough declined sharply—by 22.7 per cent over the decade as a whole. But the number of households went down less steeply, by 17.8 per cent over the ten-year period, and the numbers of one-person households actually *rose* over the decade, from 21 415 in 1961, to 23 175 in 1971 (or from 23.1 per cent to 30.1 per cent of the total number of households in the Borough) [5].

Table 4 I
Population and Household Change, 1961–71

	1961	1966	1971	% change 1961–71
Population	261 232	235 440	201 875	−22.7
Households	93 705	84 540	76 975	−17.8
One-person households	21 415	20 580	23 175	+7.0

Sources: Census data: Islington Borough Community Plan

This growth in the number of small households, which has important social consequences, affects Inner London as a whole —virtually all the areas in which one- and two-person households form more than 70 per cent of the total number of households fall in Inner London [6]. It is due to a number of different causes: the large number of pensioner households, earlier marriages, leading in turn to the earlier dissolution of existing households, and the in-migration of young single people in search of employment.

Migration particularly affects boroughs like Islington; from Census estimates it can be shown that two-thirds of all people living in the Borough in 1961 no longer lived there in 1971, having either died or moved away [7]. This loss is largely replaced—though not entirely made good—by new migrants to the Borough, in search of employment or better housing conditions.

The composition of the two streams of outward and inward migration is rather different. Of the annual outflow of 13 000 migrants in the early sixties the majority moved to the outer suburbs (particularly Enfield and Barnet) or to settlements in the Outer Metropolitan Area beyond London's Green Belt.

Outward migrants are likely to consist of population in the family-building stage of the life-cycle when the advantages of home ownership and space which the suburbs offer are particularly sought and when access to mortgages is usually easier than for older households. For the same reason the higher-income middle classes who can afford to buy easily in the suburbs have been over-represented, with a further element of skilled manual workers in engineering industries moving out with their industries to the overspill towns of Hertfordshire and Essex. In fact, 23 per cent of gross outward migration from Islington in the early sixties was to South-East England outside London, and 5 per cent of migration from the Borough was to New and Expanding Towns. The result of this net outflow of population is to open up opportunities within the housing stock for newcomers. Much of this replacement population which came into Islington during this period was from other parts of the Inner City or from overseas—of the annual inflow of 9000 migrants to Islington, 38 per cent was from other Inner London boroughs and 29 per cent from overseas.

There is another difficulty that affects both these newcomers to the Borough and the established residents, which also needs to be considered: this is the decline in the range of employment opportunities available in the Borough, especially in manufacturing industry. The loss of employment in Islington in the recent past has been very marked, and considerably greater than that in the GLC area as a whole, as Table 4 II shows:

Table 4 II

Employment in Islington and Greater London: Changes 1961–71

	Total employment	Manufacturing	Professional Services	Other Services
Greater London	−8.6%	−25.1%	+20.3%	−6.1%
Islington	−19.4%	−37.6%	+43.6%	−11.3%

In round numbers, the Borough has lost 34 000 manufacturing jobs over the past twenty years, 15 000 of them in the five years between 1966 and 1971 [8]. The effects of this change are reflected in the changes that have taken place in the socio-economic structure of the Borough's population:

Table 4 III

Percentage of economically active males, aged 15 and over, by area of usual residence and socio-economic group

SEG	Islington 1966*	1971	GLC 1971
Professional and employers/ managers (1, 2, 3, 4, 13)	8.4	11.4	19.9
Non-manual workers (5, 6)	18.4	20.8	23.5
Foremen, skilled manual and own-account workers (8, 9, 12, 14)	37.9	34.3	32.9
Semi-skilled manual and personal service workers (7, 10, 15)	18.8	18.2	13.4
Unskilled manual workers and others (11, 16, 17)	16.5	15.3	10.3

* Economically active and retired males over 15.
Source: 1966 and 1971 Census

The drop in the skilled and semi-skilled manual categories reflected in Table 4 III is of particular importance in the present context. But these figures also reflect the effects of another phenomenon of recent growth. The rise in the proportion of Islington's population in the professional and managerial category is a direct result of the process known to sociologists, in the cumbersome phrase coined by Ruth Glass, as 'gentrification'. The convenient geographical location of Islington, with good public transport services and the existence of a substantial residue of attractive Georgian and early Victorian terraced housing has drawn an element of the professional middle class back to the Inner City. One particular part of the Borough, Barnsbury, has become something of a test case of the consequences of this process for an area and its previous inhabitants. For one of the immediate results of gentrification has been to reinforce the tendency for larger property to be taken out of the rented market and revert to single-family owner-occupation. This process has been abetted by the policy of successive governments of encouraging improvement of property through substantial grants; its direct consequences can be seen in the changes that have taken place in the pattern of tenure of the Borough's housing stock.

Over the past few years, then, the population of Islington has both declined in absolute numbers and changed in composition.

This decline should, in theory, have provided the local authority with much-needed additional room for manoeuvre. However, the capacity of the housing stock is itself also in decline, as urban renewal and improvement activities take effect. Redevelopment of housing in Islington has led to an increase in the number of dwellings but a reduction in the number of rooms in the stock, since new council flats tend to be smaller than the Victorian terraces they replace. Moreover, Islington already has a high proportion of small dwellings—20.1 per cent of dwellings have one or two rooms, compared with 10.4 per cent in the GLC area as a whole. Only Camden, Kensington and Chelsea and Westminster have higher proportions of small dwellings [9]. Islington Council have calculated that rebuilding in the Borough could lead to a 20 per cent increase in the number of available dwellings between 1971 and 1981, but only a 2 per cent growth in the number of rooms.

Table 4 IV

London Borough of Islington
Projected changes in housing stock, 1971–81

1971	Dwellings stock	58 900
	Redevelopment	+14 500
	Conversions	+1560
	Slum clearance	−6670
1981	Dwellings stock	68 290

Source: Islington Council

This in turn necessarily implies a continuing fall in the population of the Borough up to the end of this decade—a prediction likely to be borne out in practice, on current (1976) trends. Further stimulus to such a fall is likely to come from the tendency for room densities to go down as smaller households increase their space requirements. Coupled with the ageing of Islington's population and the decline of the private rented sector, this should lead to a fall in the number of persons to each room in the Borough [10].

At the same time, the processes of social change referred to earlier have led to a significant shift in the distribution of households between different tenure groups, shown in the Table below:

Table 4 V

Tenure Pattern by Household: Changes 1961–71

	1961	%	1966	%	1971	%
Owner-occupied	10070	10.9	11530	13.6	10340	13.4
Local authority	15595	16.9	17250	20.4	22125	28.7
Unfurnished renting	49710	53.7	39930	47.2	28625	37.2
Furnished renting	14515	15.7	13600	16.1	14770	19.2
Other	2616	2.8	2230	2.7	1115	1.5
Total	92506	100	84540	100	76975	100

Source: Census data

The most striking change in this situation over the decade is the rapid decline in the number of households in the unfurnished rented sector. This sector has traditionally provided cheap, secure housing for the indigenous working class, in Islington as elsewhere in Inner London. At the same time, the council housing sector, which is broadly intended to cater for the same group in the population, has been growing—though at a less rapid rate. The other two sectors of the market are apparently more stable; at the top end, the growth in the owner-occupied sector has come to a halt, as the supply of cheaper housing that can be turned over from renting has dried up. The intervention of the local authority, which has also begun to purchase accommodation of this kind, has been another contributory factor in stabilizing the situation. And at the bottom end of the market, the supply of rented accommodation in the furnished sector, which was at the time of the Census not yet subject to the statutory controls over rent levels and terms of tenure that apply to the unfurnished sector, has risen slightly. It is this accommodation that has in the past catered for newcomers to London, both at the prosperous end of the market and at the poorest—it is no coincidence that ethnic minorities tend to be substantially over-represented in this sector.

The importance of tenure is underlined when we consider the distribution of adverse housing conditions between different tenure categories. The following Table shows how overcrowding and obsolescence are concentrated in particular categories—a theme we shall return to when we look in detail at the stress area.

Table 4 VI

Access to amenities by tenure, 1971

	Hot water share/ or lack	Bath share	Bath lack	Inside WC share	Inside WC lack	Overcrowded more than 1.5 persons per room
	%	%	%	%	%	%
Owner-occupiers	14.9	20.3	7.7	17.1	7.3	6.0
Renting from local authority	5.6	0.9	5.2	1.2	2.3	5.7
Unfurnished tenants	35.8	18.6	39.2	29.6	15.9	9.9
Furnished tenants	45.8	57.6	13.8	59.9	7.9	31.0
All tenures	29.0	22.7	20.9	27.7	8.8	6.6

Source: 1971 census

Much of Islington's housing is still in an appalling state. Only 51.5 per cent of Islington households had exclusive use of hot water, fixed bath and WC, one fifth (20.9 per cent) had no fixed bath or shower and almost the same number had no hot water supply. Absolute numbers are even more impressive—or devastating: 36 811 people had no access to fixed baths in Islington in 1971 and a further 37 060 shared with another household. But the Table also reveals a considerable range of provision of amenities between different tenure categories. Council tenants are far better off than any other tenure group— even owner-occupiers. Nearly all council tenants had exclusive use of a fixed bath, compared to 70 per cent of owner-occupiers, just over 40 per cent unfurnished tenants and just over a quarter furnished tenants. Although furnished tenants were generally the worst off as far as access to amenities was concerned, unfurnished tenants had more restricted access to a bath, since 39.2 per cent of unfurnished tenants had no access to a bath at all, compared with only 13.8 per cent of furnished tenants. This indicates that unfurnished tenants lived in a different type of dwelling—cottages rather than a large dwelling converted into many units—or dwellings that had had a different type of management—possibly landlords unable to afford improvements, such as bathroom installations, rather than landlords with no cash flow problem and a policy of improvement in order to raise rents. We shall return to this point when we come to consider reasons why unfurnished rather than furnished tenants appear to wish to move from Islington. Meanwhile, the important point to note is that if one wants to be decently housed—in terms of amenities—in Islington, then one should become a council tenant.

Similarly, severe overcrowding (more than $1\frac{1}{2}$ persons per room) was greatest among households in the furnished rented sector. However, if the opposite end of the spectrum is examined, least overcrowding—or, some would say, 'worst under-occupation'—occurred in the owner-occupied sector where one third of households lived at less than 0.5 persons per room.

These data help to underline a number of points. First, in Islington the major housing problem is one of the old age of the housing stock, which is indicated by the figures for lack of amenities. These problems are compounded by the size of the stock. Severe overcrowding, while still a problem, affects fewer households, although the Borough has estimated in its Community Plan that 22 000 people (11.5 per cent of the total population) fall into this category. Secondly, the differences in occupancy rates between furnished and unfurnished private tenants and the similarities between unfurnished and council tenants suggest that furnished and unfurnished tenants tend to have different characteristics: they are different-sized households, they live in different types of dwelling units, they probably came to Islington at different times—for example, many of the furnished tenants may have arrived after the controls introduced in the 1965 Rent Act began to 'bite' into the unfurnished sector. We shall be able to test some of these propositions in later chapters—and it is vital that we do, for the apparent differences between the dwelling type occupied by furnished and unfurnished tenants have important implications for our main theme.

Implications for Mobility

To provide the context for discussion of who moves within and beyond Islington, and, in particular, to New and Expanding Towns, it is important to establish what opportunities there are for people to better their housing. The concept of 'intervening opportunities' used in migration theory provides a useful framework for such a discussion [11]. This concept has both physical

and psychological connotations. For example, people who consider moving from location A to location B may find suitable
accommodation *before* they get to point B; in this case the location
they finally settle on is called an 'intervening opportunity'
because it intervened physically between opportunities—or lack
of them—in A and the opportunities for relocation in B. But
such a concept can also be used in a hierarchy of housing values.
That is, people perceive their location A as undesirable in some
way, and, at the same time, perceive location B as the ideal.
However, if for some reason—financial, for example—they
cannot achieve location B, then they will settle for location C
which represents a compromise between constraints and opportunities, and in the sense that it is 'second best' in a hierarchy
of housing values represents a psychological 'intervening opportunity'.

In the following sections, New and Expanding Towns will
be treated as an 'intervening opportunity' in this latter sense.
That is, we shall be looking at the opportunities Islington
residents who currently live in poor housing have to better their
housing in or around the area of the London Borough of
Islington on the assumption that if such housing were available,
people would not move out to New or Expanding Towns. This
may, of course, be the reverse of the truth. It may be that a
New or Expanding Town, so far from being 'second best' in
a hierarchy of housing values, is actually the ideal location for
many Islington residents and that decent housing in Islington
is an 'intervening opportunity' for those, such as unskilled
workers, who have great difficulty in moving out to a New Town.
These are questions that we shall consider further in Chapter
6; meanwhile we turn to look at opportunities for decent housing
in Islington, without speculating—except in passing—on those
to whom those opportunities might appeal.

The Range of Opportunities for Islington Residents

In theory, the range of opportunities available, at the time when
we undertook our survey, to Islington residents wishing to
improve their housing circumstances was quite wide. In practice,
choice was severely restricted. At the upper end of the market,
owner-occupation within Islington was by then almost completely out of the reach of working-class families who wish to

purchase a house and live in it themselves without letting off to tenants. Damp, but roomy, Edwardian terraced houses in North Islington (the area studied in the stress area survey) were still for sale in 1974 at about £13 000, but restrictions on lending by Building Societies effectively ruled them out for those with gross incomes of less than £4500 a year. Private houses in parts of suburbia, however, may be more readily accessible to working-class families with lower incomes; certainly migration data indicate that some London families find their way out to the fringe of London and into owner-occupation. However, those who succeed in moving in this way will remain, for broad economic reasons, a minority.

The range of effective choice for working-class residents (and newcomers) is therefore limited to the public sector, or to opportunities provided by public intervention in the private sector. As we have seen, local authority housing already caters for nearly a third of the Borough's population, and this proportion is continuously rising as a result of an extensive public sector building programme. By the early 1980s Islington Borough expect to own nearly half the housing stock in the authority's area. Despite this effort, however, there are no signs that the Borough's waiting list for housing in Islington will shrink. The rate of obsolescence, the progressive disappearance of the privately rented sector, the pattern of migration in and out of the Borough, the problem of land availability which means that land must be cleared and people rehoused before housing becomes available for waiting-list applicants, the availability of housing advice, all combine to elongate the waiting list. In 1972, there were 11 509 families on the waiting list, of whom the Borough estimated that just over 9300 were genuinely waiting for council accommodation [12]. In the same year, 1443 dwellings were available in Islington for letting by the Borough (only half of these arose from new building; the rest came from re-lets or other sources). During that year, 1313 families were rehoused by the Borough not because they were on the waiting list but because they had been displaced by the Borough's own activities, for example, slum clearance, improvement, road schemes and provision for open space. Thus Islington itself could only house 130 families off the waiting list in the whole year, despite the completion of 708 new dwellings and vacancies in a further 579 dwellings [13].

However, Islington is not the only authority that provides public housing for Islington residents. The 1963 London Government Act provided for two kinds of housing authority in London: the local boroughs as primary agencies and the Greater London Council as the strategic authority. There have, in the past, been attempts to divest the GLC of its pool of houses and hand them over to the boroughs in which the dwellings are sited, but until the 1977 elections the GLC intended to keep control of its existing estates pending an agreement with the boroughs on a strategic housing policy for London as a whole.

The GLC's contribution to Inner London's housing problems is an important one, since it allocates the greater part of its own redevelopment and building efforts to the Inner Boroughs. During the period under review, 88 per cent of the annual stock of vacancies available to the Council were used for Inner London purposes—an average of about 20 000 dwellings a year. Put another way, more than one-third of the municipal housing available to the Inner Boroughs each year was supplied by the GLC.

The assistance provided by the GLC in the inner boroughs has taken three different forms: direct provision of new housing, through construction of dwellings (the GLC has a number of major schemes in Islington); allocation of vacancies in existing GLC properties within Islington and in other parts of London through the nomination scheme; and access to housing in New or Expanding Towns through NETS (the process described in detail in Chapter 3).

The nomination system established by the GLC and London Boroughs consists of a complex series of management and allocation procedures, by which families are given access to municipal housing owned by the GLC or to Borough housing outside their own area of residence. The nucleus of the system is the GLC's own stock of dwellings, spread geographically over the London conurbation (188 000 in 1977). In addition to vacancies arising in this stock, and to new building of approximately 5000 dwellings a year, the GLC also has nomination rights over a limited number of council dwellings owned by the Boroughs, mostly in outer London, which are surplus to local needs. In this way, Islington was able in 1972 to obtain access to 750 lettings for their own cases—although there is, of course, no guarantee that these dwellings will be re-let to Islington families, since they are not part of the Islington Borough's housing stock. This contribution obviously represents a considerable relief for hard-pressed Inner London boroughs; to some extent, it also provides Inner Londoners with an opportunity to move out of their borough without necessarily changing their jobs—as they would probably have to do if they moved to a New or Expanding Town.

The range of opportunities opened up by this scheme is determined by the location of the stock itself. Of all dwellings owned by the GLC when we conducted our survey, 60 per cent were located in the inner boroughs (Group A) (just under 3 per cent in Islington), 27 per cent in the outer London boroughs (Group B) and 13 per cent outside the Greater London area. Thus it is no surprise that of the families rehoused through nomination schemes between 1965 and the time of our study, 24 per cent remained in the same borough (being transferred to local GLC estates); 44 per cent were rehoused in another Inner London borough, and only 27 per cent were housed in outer London. In all, some 1300 families moved from inner boroughs each year to the suburbs through the nomination scheme. A further 1000 families transferred from GLC properties that they already occupied in Inner London to outer London estates; these vacated properties are then re-allocated by the GLC. On average, therefore, 2300 families from Inner London moved within the public sector to the suburbs each year, or about 7000 people in all.

Within the private rented sector, where the largest proportion of Islington residents still live, there is another way available to them to better their housing. This is if they are tenants living in a dwelling that is improved, either under the provisions of the 1969 Housing Act or the 1974 Housing Act (which came into force after the period we studied); the former gives grants for improvement of individual houses while the latter gives grants for the improvement of dwellings and environmental conditions in areas declared as Housing Action Areas. The provisions of the 1974 Act are the result, at least in part, of the relative failure of earlier legislation to benefit those most in need. Data referring to improvement grants for the year 1972 and the declaration of General Improvement Areas under the 1969 Housing Act have been published by the GLC and generally tend to substantiate those criticisms. In 1972, most improvement grants given in Islington went to owner-occupiers (105 out of 176), while the majority of conversion grants went to private owners of property they did not then occupy (351 out of 516). The local authority received 42 conversion and improvement grants and housing associations received 90 conversion and improvement grants. In addition, Islington had only declared one General Improvement Area between 1969 and 1972. It contained 160 dwellings; only Tower Hamlets had a smaller improvement area programme in 1972 [14]. The pattern seems clear; improvement and conversion grants were on the whole used in 1972 by those who were probably already well-placed in the housing market—either owner-occupiers improving their own dwellings or property developers converting dwellings into smaller units in order to make a profit. It is unlikely that many of the genuinely badly housed benefited from this programme in 1972.

This review has tended to support the proposition that the opportunities available to ordinary Islington residents to improve their housing are limited. In practice, they amount to the following: house purchase on the edges of London; gaining an Islington council dwelling by living in a redevelopment area or coming to the top of an extremely long housing waiting list —of these last two, the former opportunity is, to some extent, a matter of chance and one's opportunities for rehousing are still governed by strict eligibility rules, while the latter can mean an intolerably long wait; gaining a GLC dwelling by living in a GLC redevelopment area or being nominated off the waiting list by Islington Borough for GLC or outer borough accommodation; finally, living in a GIA or Housing Action Area and benefiting from improvement without having to move. As we have seen, the chances for each family that wishes to better their housing of any one of these events actually taking place are highly restricted.

From the discussion in this chapter of housing conditions and opportunities within and beyond Islington we can draw the following conclusions: that about half Islington households lack the exclusive use of an important amenity, and that the numbers on the housing waiting list are very considerable and continuously growing. Islington's new housing programme, although substantial, cannot keep up with the pressure of demand for housing in the public sector. As a result, Islington Council is highly dependent on the housing contribution made by the GLC, either directly or through the nomination scheme. The prospects, therefore, for those Islington residents who wish to better their housing and stay in or near Islington are not hopeful. A major issue we have not yet investigated, however, is how well placed Islington residents are to move to a New or Expanding Town if they find they cannot obtain decent housing in Islington. In particular, do they have the skills that are virtually essential for workers to move through the NETS?

References

1. *Greater London Transportation Study income data* (GLC 1971).

2. *Greater London Development Plan: report of Studies*, op. cit., section 2.70.

3. *Tomorrow in Upper Holloway*. A Plan for Area Improvement. North Islington Housing Rights Project: Report 1 (Shelter, 1973); *Priorities for Housing Action*. North Islington Housing Rights Project: Report 2 (Shelter, 1973).

4. London Borough of Islington, *Housing Needs 1971–81* (unpublished 1972).

5. Islington Borough Community Plan, *Topic Paper No. 5 (Housing)* (Islington Borough Council, 1973).

6. Greater London Council, *Housing Facts and Figures* (GLC 1973), figure 12.

7. Islington Borough Community Plan, *Topic Paper No. 5*, op. cit.

8. Islington Borough Community Plan, *Topic Paper No. 6 (Employment)* (Islington Borough Council, 1973), p. 4.

9. Islington Borough Community Plan, *Topic Paper No. 5 (Housing)*, op. cit., p. 5.

10. PERETZ, J. and DAVIES, H., 'Demographic factors and borough occupancy rates', *Quarterly Bulletin of the Intelligence Unit*, GLC, No. 10, March 1970.

11. See LEE, EVERETT, 'A theory of migration' in JACKSON, J. A. (ed.), *Migration* (Cambridge University Press, 1969).

12. *Annual Abstract of Greater London Statistics*, Volume 7, 1972 (Greater London Council, 1973), Table 8.13.

13. *Annual Abstract of Greater London Statistics*, op. cit., Table 8.04.

14. *Annual Abstract of Greater London Statistics*, op. cit., Table 8.11.

Chapter Five

Living in a Stress Area[1]

In order to fill in the general picture of life in an Inner Borough with detailed evidence on the housing circumstances, skills and kinship patterns of people living in conditions of housing stress, a social survey was carried out in one of the less prosperous parts of Islington. The area chosen was the one known as Tollington, in the north eastern part of the Borough [1]. The housing there consists predominantly of late Victorian terraced houses, originally intended for occupation by single families: somewhat depressed—if less pretentious—cousins of the villas once inhabited by Mr Pooter and his friends, a mile or so to the west. These houses have mostly declined, over time, into multi-occupation, either in flats through token conversion or as straightforward lodging-houses. However, they are supplemented in the important function that they still perform of providing cheap accommodation, by a number of smaller artisan cottages, some of them still rented for single-family occupation. More recently, numbers of both kinds of houses have been demolished to make way for local authority housing, of a straight-forward—if rather depressingly unimaginative—kind; others await a similar fate, shrouded in corrugated iron. Occasional bright splashes of paint show where the odd dwelling has been handed over, as a 'short-life' property to a local group, or simply squatted in, without benefit of formal arrangements. But in

---

[1] This chapter, like some parts of Chapter Four, draws very largely on work done by Garry McDonald, who was responsible within the project for the stress area survey. Some of this work has been published elsewhere as: 'Metropolitan Housing Policy and the Stress Areas', *Urban Studies*, 1974, **11**, 27–37.

general the environment is drab; exteriors mostly long un-
painted, except where one of the new wave of owner-occupiers
from overseas has painstakingly picked out the decorative stucco
with fresh colours. Litter swirls along the pavement where the
children play (Islington has less recreational open space than
any other Inner London borough).

But, despite its depressed outward appearance, the area has
enjoyed, in the past at least, two substantial assets: reasonable
access to employment, and cheap and secure housing. Only
comparatively recently have these two assets been threatened
by the processes of change now taking place in the Inner City.
In this respect—as in others—the area seems sufficiently typical
of the less privileged part of the Borough to enable us to draw
valid conclusions about the situation in which the Inner
London working class lives, and the extent to which there are
realistic alternatives open to them, in attempting to improve
their situation.

The sample was drawn from a population of four polling
districts in the Highbury and Parkway wards of Tollington.
The sampling frame employed for selecting addresses was the
Electoral Register. A sample of 704 addresses was drawn, after
adjustments; 512 usable interviews (a 73 per cent response rate)
were obtained. There have been important changes recently in
the area as a result of population mobility and urban renewal
which make the Tollington district a significant area of social
transition. The most visible of these changes dominate the local
landscape in the shape of new municipal tower blocks in North
Highbury and in the Station ward adjoining. This is the location
of over a third of new house-building by the Borough and the
GLC since these new authorities came into existence in 1965,
and it is forecast that 30 per cent of the properties in the
Tollington district will have been redeveloped by them in 1981.
One of the positive advantages of redevelopment here is the
relatively low density of much of the older residential areas where
there was a good deal of small terraced housing in single-
family occupation. Rebuilding can provide a significant gain
in the density of dwelling units—a windfall which is increasingly
rare in the Inner City.

The other major process of change is through migration. As
we have already seen, Islington has experienced a sharp fall in
population due to outward migration, accelerating over the

past decade. This high degree of mobility has also affected the Tollington district.

People in the Study Area

The extent of the social changes that have resulted from the twin processes of urban renewal and selective migration were among the most graphic findings in our survey, and a brief summary of these provides a setting for more detailed analysis of groups within the sample which follows. First of all, the sample showed a bias towards working-class households in social classes IV and V—the semi-skilled and unskilled occupations. Forty-five per cent of all heads of households were in these two social classes, compared with only 24 per cent of all economically active males in London in 1971. Unlike some of the wards where gentrification has occurred, Parkway and North Highbury are very clearly areas of working-class settlement with a marked under-representation not only of the professional and intermediate workers, but, to a lesser extent, of the skilled 'middle-mass' in the class structure [2].

Table 5 I

Socio-economic groups in the GLC, Islington and the stress area (percentages)

SEG	GLC 1971*	Islington 1971*	Stress Area residents 1972†	
Professional and employers/ managers (1, 2, 3, 4, 13)	19.9	11.4	3.3	
Non-manual workers (5, 6)	23.5	20.8	23.3	
Foremen, skilled manual and own-account workers (8, 9, 12, 14)	32.9	34.3	27.6	
Semi-skilled manual and personal service workers (7, 10, 15)	13.4	18.2	27.4	
Unskilled manual workers and others (11, 16, 17)	10.3	15.3	18.6	
Total	100	100	100	(512)

* Economically active males aged 15 and over
† Heads of household
Sources: 1971 Census and Stress Area Survey

A substantial proportion of the local working class is now drawn from the various ethnic minorities, as a result of post-war immigration to London: 36 per cent of household heads were born outside the United Kingdom and, with their families, they formed nearly half the total population recorded in the sample. The most important ethnic groups were migrants from Eire, Greek Cypriots and West Indians, in that order. In addition, there was a substantial population of miscellaneous European and African and Asian origin. The British-born population could itself be split into two categories; natives born in the Inner London boroughs who formed 35 per cent of the sample and the 'non-locals' from outer London and the provinces who made up the remainder.

Table 5 II

Birthplace of stress area sample and Islington residents (percentages)

	Islington	Stress area residents	
England	71.5	63.6	26.2 Islington 19.8 Elsewhere in London 17.6 Elsewhere in UK
Rest of UK	3.8		
Eire	6.4	11.9	
West Indies	3.6	7.0	
Cyprus	3.9	5.3	
Rest of New Commonwealth	3.7	1.8	
Others	6.7	10.3	
Total	100	100	

Sources: Census and Stress Area Survey

The sample had been a very mobile one. Half of all households had moved into their present accommodation in the previous five years and two-thirds had moved at least once in the past decade. Two-thirds of previous moves had been from within Islington and 90 per cent originated within Inner London. This extensive but localized mobility appears to be the result of upward filtering in the housing stock, stimulated both by the exodus of the original population from the area and by redevelopment in Tollington.

Housing

As we saw in the previous chapter, one of the most important factors that help to determine an individual's housing conditions is the tenure of the dwelling he lives in. Tenure, in turn, is usually assumed to reflect the social class to which he belongs; all other thing being equal, the owner-occupier (in London) is likely to be—by aspiration, at least—middle-class, and the council house tenant working-class. Only the private rented sector caters for a wider variety of people, from the single-pensioner households, the poorest of all, to the ambitious young middle-class birds of passage—the sociologists' 'spiralists'.

But in the study area, these links between tenure and social class are not as close as usual. Table 5 III gives the breakdown of the sample by tenure; it is followed by a discussion of each group, showing who lives in what kind of housing in Tollington.

Table 5 III

Tenure: Islington and stress area (percentages)

	Islington 1971	Stress area 1972
Owner-occupied	13.4	26.7
Renting from local authority	28.7	22.5
Renting privately		
unfurnished	37.2	32.9
furnished	19.2	15.5
Other	1.4	2.2
Total	100	100

Sources: Census and Stress Area Survey

Owner-occupiers

Just over a quarter of the households in the sample were owner-occupiers at the time of the survey; they lived mainly in the small artisan cottages which still survive in the district but which are in urgent need of modernization or replacement. There is an important dichotomy within the owner-occupier group.

The first element consists of the 41 per cent who owned their homes outright and had lived in their present homes for over ten years, forming one of the most stable elements in the local population. The second element among the owner-occupiers is a new one: the ethnic minorities, who are in fact the only birthplace group to be significantly over-represented in this tenure. Half of this group—principally West Indians and Cypriots—are buying or own their homes, compared with about 20 per cent of those from other birthplaces. This recent inflow of ethnic minorities into owner-occupation has been largely out of furnished tenancies and accounts for three-quarters of new purchasers since 1962. A substantial number of these new buyers have raised GLC or Islington mortgages (41 per cent) and their presence in this sector explains the high proportion of young families who are owner-occupiers. The basic division among owner-occupiers is therefore between the long-established, geographically stable English whose children are leaving or have left home, and who own their homes outright, and newcomers from Cyprus and the West Indies with young children, who are buying properties on a mortgage.

Council tenants

The new Islington Council estate at Harvist Road in the study area is only part of the much more extensive redevelopment activity taking place locally. Station Ward, adjoining the study area, has been virtually rebuilt as a result of the construction of the new GLC estate at Alsen Road and the Islington Borough estate at Poole's Park. One obvious consequence of these changes has been to reduce the stock of privately owned dwellings in the area. Another has been to make local authority housing the most desirable form of housing, in terms of the relationship between levels of rent and standards. However, access to council housing has been restricted by the Council's rules of eligibility which, until 1970, excluded furnished tenants from rehousing obligations, on grounds of their transience. The majority of new entrants to council housing in Tollington during the last decade had therefore been unfurnished tenants or council tenants transferring from other areas.

As a result of the pattern of selection for entry into council housing, this sector has been dominated by the local working class and, in consequence, contains a bias towards older families and retired households. These are the groups most likely to score high points for local residence and length on the council waiting list and to have been in unfurnished tenancies. Unfurnished tenants are the group most likely to be rehoused by the Council from clearance areas—unlike owner-occupiers who often accept compensation for their property and move off to buy similar housing somewhere else. Unfurnished tenants also form the majority of families on the waiting list.

Just as striking as the bias towards the older, indigenous working class in council housing is the tendency for this sector to house a disproportionately low number of young, growing, families. Of the various ethnic minorities, only the Irish appear to have penetrated council housing at all effectively; this probably reflects their earlier settlement in Islington and the higher proportion formerly living in unfurnished dwellings, and counterbalances the relatively low entry of the Irish into home ownership. The small proportion of young families in council housing reflects the problems confronting newly married couples generally in the Inner City, who face long delays before they are eligible for council accommodation. As we have seen, young families tend to be drawn from the ethnic minorities, living in furnished accommodation and oriented, either by choice or constraint, towards home ownership. These minorities are very substantially under-represented in local authority accommodation, to an extent that can only partly be explained by their recent arrival.

Unfurnished tenants

This group is the largest of the tenure categories in the stress area—just under a third of the sample in all. They are among the most stable and longest established residents in the survey area. This situation is chiefly the result of rent control legislation which has ensured low rents and security of tenure in this sector. The same Acts which guaranteed these basic rights for existing tenants also made these tenancies less accessible to future arrivals, since landlords tended to convert vacated unfurnished tenancies to furnished tenure in order to avoid these restrictions, or sell them off at the earliest opportunity in order to realize their assets and invest them in more profitable ways. The bias in this sector is therefore towards retired households and older, childless couples, with a marked under-representation of young families. There is an equally strong bias away from recently arrived ethnic minorities, of whom only 10 per cent are unfurnished tenants, compared with 41 per cent among indigenous Inner Londoners and the same proportion of the Irish.

Furnished tenants

Furnished tenants made up 16 per cent of all households in the sample. The furnished sector contains the most geographically mobile population—43 per cent of households in this sector had lived in their accommodation less than one year—and provide the main point of entry into the Borough for migrant households. Hence the high concentrations of ethnic minorities (including the Irish) in this form of housing and the very low proportion of local English. In all, 30 per cent of ethnic minorities are furnished tenants compared with only 2 per cent of the local English. For the same reason, there is a large concentration of single persons and young families in furnished accommodation. This sector is not only a point of entry to the Inner City, but also a staging post: furnished tenants moving on have formed the majority of first-time buyers and of new tenants of unfurnished properties during the last decade. Within the study area, this movement has been dominated by the ethnic minorities.

Conditions in the Stress Area

How do the different tenures differ in terms of the quality of housing that they provide?

The main indices of housing stress in the sample were the sharing of dwellings in multi-occupation and the consequences of this sharing. In the sample as a whole, over half (55 per cent) of households lived in shared accommodation and it is clear that deficiencies in basic amenities were the most common result of sharing in the private sector; but they also occurred in substandard terraced housing which was owned and occupied by single households. In all, 53 per cent of households did not have the sole use of an inside WC—a worse situation than in the

Borough as a whole, where 37 per cent of households were in this position in 1971. Similarly, slightly fewer households had sole use of a fixed bath or shower than in Islington as a whole.

But when the different tenure groups are examined, striking differences, in terms of amenity and overcrowding, emerge. Table 5 IV describes the differences in tenure groups.

Table 5 IV

Percentages of households in the stress area sample with sole use of certain amenities, by tenure group

	Inside WC	Sole use of fixed bath/ shower	Piped hot water
All tenures	53	48	73
Owner-occupiers	57	52	85
Council tenants	94	95	96
Private rented			
unfurnished	41	29	53
furnished	14	15	62

Source: Stress Area Survey

It is clear from Table 5 IV that council tenants are in the most favourable position as far as domestic amenities are concerned: all but about 5 per cent have exclusive use of an inside WC, fixed bath or shower and piped hot water. Households in the private sector fall substantially below these standards, as might be expected. The majority of local authority dwellings have been built since 1965 to Parker Morris standards and are subsidized through the rates and Exchequer while, by comparison, dwellings in the private sector were mostly built in the nineteenth century and their owners have not had the resources or the disposition to maintain or improve them to contemporary standards of fitness.

Owner-occupiers have the highest standards of basic domestic provision in the private sector but they are, nevertheless, a deprived group by comparison with council tenants. Just over half have exclusive use of an inside WC and a fixed bath or shower—which emphasizes the poor standards of the old terraced housing in much of Tollington and the enormous potential for home improvement here. But the worst conditions of all are in the private rented sector, and here the problems are even more complex. Unfurnished tenants tend to fare better than furnished tenants, largely because they more often live in cottage-style self-contained accommodation. Even so, 59 per cent of unfurnished tenants do not have sole use of an inside WC and 71 per cent do not have their own washing facilities. The lowest standards of all occurred in the furnished sector where accommodation is almost entirely shared with other households. Whereas basic domestic amenities can be installed relatively easily in owner-occupied housing, in the rented sector much of the basic deprivation is a result of sharing of facilities and its removal requires extensive conversion of properties into self-contained units—or their demolition.

The second primary cause of housing stress after sharing of dwellings in Tollington is overcrowding. Nearly half the households lived at densities of more than one person to a living room and a quarter lived under conditions of serious overcrowding, at densities of over one and a half persons per room. Here, the incidence of deprivation is different from the pattern observed for sharing of amenities. Considering first the favourable end of the spectrum, the lowest room densities occur in the furnished sector, where 93 per cent of households live at one or fewer people per room, while the three remaining tenures cluster at around the 50 per cent level. At the other extreme, owner-occupiers and unfurnished tenants are the most overcrowded groups; almost one in three of both these groups live at very high densities. But council tenants are not far behind, with just over a quarter living at more than 1.5 persons per room.

In summary, while council tenants are overwhelmingly the best off for amenities, furnished tenants appear to have more living space. Larger households tend, as might be expected, to be the most crowded: 90 per cent of two-person families lived at densities of one person or less per room compared with only 33 per cent of large households with five or more members. However, these large families tend to be among the recent arrivals to the area, and the fact that such families initially find their accommodation in the furnished rented sector tends to compensate for this tendency towards overcrowding. It also helps to account for the finding—which runs counter to other recent experience—that members of the ethnic minority groups are less overcrowded than those born in Inner London.

Employment and Social Class

The most important finding under this head was that nearly two-thirds of the household heads who were economically active were in manual occupations. However, there were some significant differences between social groups in their pattern of skills (see Table 5 V). Among the economically active heads of households, almost half the English workers born outside Inner London were in non-manual occupations (social class I–II) compared to 30 per cent of local English-born and 20 per cent of the ethnic minorities.

Table 5 V
Social class of household heads in full-time employment by birthplace (percentages)

Social class	Whole sample	Inner London	Non-Locals	Irish	Ethnic Minority Groups
I–II Non-manual	31	30	47	22	20
III Skilled manual	26	29	19	24	32
IV Semi-skilled	25	20	19	28	33
V Unskilled	14	18	11	20	8
Others	4	3	4	6	7
Totals	100%	100%	100%	100%	100%
Base	343	98	100	46	99

Source: Stress Area Survey

There is clearly a substantial element of young, career-orientated migrants among these non-locals, mainly recent newcomers to Islington, living in private rented accommodation. The next highest proportion of skilled workers was among local English-born in Inner London, while the ethnic groups contained the lowest proportion of non-manual workers. The highest concentrations of the semi- and unskilled manual workers, taken together, were found among the Irish; almost half of Irish heads of household were in semi-skilled or unskilled occupations, compared with 39 per cent in the sample as a whole. Among the ethnic minorities, a third were in semi-skilled employment— the highest proportion of all the different groups; interestingly, however, there was an exceptionally low representation of the totally unskilled in these groups (8 per cent) and a slightly higher than average proportion of skilled (32 per cent). This suggests that they could be marginally better placed when it comes to looking for alternative jobs in a different labour market —for example, in a New or Expanding Town.

As one would expect, these findings have important implications for income levels in Tollington. Among full-time workers the highest earnings were achieved by skilled manual workers of whom 36 per cent earned over £30 per week (in April 1971), compared with only 26 per cent of non-manual workers. The majority of the latter were in routine clerical jobs, which are generally lower-paid than such skilled manual occupations as drivers, electricians, bricklayers and so on. The lowest wages were found among the unskilled workers, half of whom earned less than £20 a week. The next lowest-paid were workers in service and semi-skilled occupations (assemblers, bus conductors, porters and waiters).

An important reason for the low levels of earnings in the sample was the large proportion of workers in low-status, low-skilled jobs; but equally crucial was the fact that the majority of workers were employed in the service industries and specifically in some of the lowest-paid sectors of these industries. Nearly half of the sample worked in local government, transport and distribution, hotels, catering and other miscellaneous personal services. Only 20 per cent were employed in manufacturing, where earnings for skilled and part-skilled workers tend to be higher than in the less productive service industries.

Earnings in the sample were still further depressed by the fact that almost a third of all heads of household were not in full-time employment at the time of the survey. This figure is made up of retired household heads (10 per cent) and non-active heads aged below 65 (21 per cent). The majority of the latter were unsupported mothers or widows. The variations between different groups—especially allowing for the likely unreliability of the income data—were not great; the categories with consistently lower income were those, as could be predicted, with a particularly high proportion of non-active households.

In general, low incomes are a problem facing the whole spectrum of social groups in Tollington and, while there are observable clusterings of high and low earners, these are a result of marginal fluctuations. No one group can be isolated as being a typically high-income sector of the population, although retired and single-person households are clearly typically poor.

Kinship

We looked particularly at the significance of the extended family for people in the study area, since previous research has drawn attention to the importance of this factor as a deterrent to mobility among working-class people, and to the very significant effect of mobility on kinship patterns, when it does take place.

Tollington contains a large number of small households and correspondingly fewer nuclear family groups; in fact, 60 per cent of households consisted of one or two persons (Table 5 VI) and the average household size was 2.7 persons. This bias towards small households is of growing significance in Inner City areas, as we saw in the previous chapter. Three categories of small households were found in the Tollington sample: childless couples, whose children had left home; pensioner households and single people living alone. These three groups accounted for most of the one- and two-person households in the area: the residual element consisted of students and young workers sharing accommodation. The largest concentration of small households occurs among those headed by English not born locally; 71 per cent of these contain one or two persons—a slightly higher proportion than among those headed by Inner Londoners, among whom older, smaller households predominate. The nuclear families consisting of parents and children at home formed only 36 per cent of the total sample and the majority of these were young, expanding families in which the eldest child was still under 16.

The relatively low proportion of family groups in the sample is a reflection of the social character of North Islington and its function as an area of transition, within the Inner City. By comparison, 54 per cent of households in more stable and homogeneous Bethnal Green were family groups while for the Borough of Swansea the figure was 51 per cent [3].

Increasingly, the nuclear family in Tollington is likely to belong to one of the ethnic minorities who have moved into the area over the past decade. Only a quarter of English-born households are nuclear families, compared with over half of Irish and overseas-born households. The latter also tend to have larger

Table 5 VI

Household composition in the stress area (percentages)

Nuclear families	
Young families (parent/s with unmarried children, eldest child under 16)	24
Older families (parent/s with married children, or youngest child over 15)	12
Childless couples	
aged over 45 (married couples living alone in which head of household 45–64)	14
aged under 45 (married couples living alone in which head of household under 45)	8
Retired households	
single person (persons living alone over 65)	6
couples (married couples, living alone, in which head of household 65+)	4
Single-person households	19
under 65 (persons living alone under 65)	19
Others (households, including households with adults related to rest of household but not children of the head of the household, or non-family groups)	13
Total	100%

Source: Stress Area Survey (for definitions, see Appendix 2)

average sizes of household: the average household with head born in Inner London consists of 2.1 persons, compared with 4.2 among the Greek Cypriots at the other extreme.

All this has important consequences for the geographical pattern of relationships between members of the extended family (Table 5 VII).

The survey data show that only a minority of the sample have parents or children living in the Islington area; it is brothers and sisters who are most frequently found locally. However, weekly contact tends to be least frequent with brothers and sisters living locally and is strongest with parents and children. Of those questioned, 91 per cent with children in the Borough maintain contact with them weekly, at least, compared with 76 per cent of those with parents living locally and only 59 per cent of those with local brothers or sisters. This pattern of closer relationship with children holds good even in cases where they live at a greater geographical distance; as large a proportion of respondents with children living in South-East England (outside

Greater London) had weekly contact with them as that which maintained weekly contact with brothers and sisters in other London boroughs.

Table 5 VII

Geographical distribution of extended family (percentage of ethnic groups)

	Natives of Inner London	Non- Locals	Minority Ethnic groups*	Whole sample	Weekly contact†
Children in					
Islington	16	9	2	9	91
London	22	22	8	17	61
South-East	31	15	4	17	32
Brothers or sisters in					
Islington	45	29	38	38	59
London	52	41	39	44	34
South-East	50	40	18	35	9
Parents in					
Islington	18	11	9	13	76
London	10	11	8	9	53
South-East	6	5	2	4	22

* Including Irish
† Per cent of subjects with kin in each area maintaining weekly contact
Source: Stress Area Survey

The Potential for Mobility

Finally, what implications do the findings of the stress area survey have for possible movement to a New or Expanding Town? Two elements in the situation are of particular importance: the skills possessed by potential migrants, and their housing circumstances. Not unusually for this policy area, these two factors tend to pull in different directions.

In terms of the potential for movement to employment in a New or Expanding Town, the most important information is contained in Table 5 V, which describes the social class of economically active heads of household. A high proportion of these household heads were in manual occupations—just over a quarter of them in skilled manual jobs. It is this latter group of skilled workers who would presumably have the easiest passage to a New or Expanding Town. At the other extreme, one-third of the stress area sample were not economically active at all, and unless they were the parents of Development Corporation tenants (and very few indeed were likely to fall into this category) then this group had absolutely no chance of moving to a New or Expanding Town. In between, there is a further substantial category of semi-skilled workers (exactly a quarter of the sample), who might qualify under other circumstances. One point worth underlining is that the ethnic minorities contained the largest proportion of skilled manual workers of any of the birthplace groups.

At the same time, the housing situation in the stress area imposes further, and different, limitations. The sector likely to contain the highest proportion of the potentially mobile is the furnished rented sector—the sector containing the highest proportion of newcomers and providing the least security for its occupants. The data confirm that this is the case; but the two groups that might furnish significant numbers of migrants—the ethnic minorities and the young, higher-paid newcomers to the Borough—seem, for different reasons, unlikely to take advantage of the opportunities that their skills confer, and move to a New or Expanding Town. The minorities, as the discussion earlier in this chapter suggests, have alternative opportunities for mobility, in terms of movement into owner-occupation; and owner-occupation, in turn, implies a commitment to a particular house and a specific locality that is likely to be an enduring one. Similarly, the younger newcomers are likely to see their future in terms of progress in the white collar employment that originally drew them to the neighbourhood and their housing will be valued for the propinquity it provides to such employment. Islington, with its easy access to the expanding market for office jobs in the City, has obvious attractions not shared by most Expanding Towns.

Such movement as does take place from the Tollington stress area to the New and Expanding Towns therefore seems likely to be from among the occupants of council housing or the unfurnished rented sector—both groups enjoy a substantial measure of security, and some protection, at least, against rising costs. Both these are factors that might be thought likely to deter the intending migrant; though to what extent, the data from the stress area study do not make clear. In order to elucidate the importance of housing—and other factors like the availability of relevant information—we turn in the next chapter to considering the evidence from another part of the study, about those who have actually taken the decision to move.

References

1. London Borough of Islington Planning Department, *Tollington Study* (1969)

2. Greater London Council. Dept of Planning and Transportation, Research Report No. 5, *Characteristics of London's households 1967* (GLC 1970).

3. YOUNG, M. and WILLMOTT, P., op. cit., ROSSER, C. and HARRIS, C., *The family and social change* (Routledge and Kegan Paul, 1965).

Chapter Six

Moving from Islington

How far can the problems encountered by the inhabitants of deprived areas like Tollington, and described in the last chapter, be relieved by planned migration to New and Expanding Towns? The evidence on which this chapter is based comes from a survey of migrants to New and Expanding Towns from Islington. These respondents were a sample of people who had moved to New and Expanding Towns from the London Borough of Islington between 1967 and mid-1972 through the Industrial Selection Scheme (now NETS). They included those who had moved with their firms and those who had voluntarily registered on the Scheme. The methodology of the survey is covered in more detail in Appendix 2; but altogether 201 respondents living in ten New and Expanding Towns were interviewed. We have also used data from the survey of the Islington stress area described in the previous chapter in order to draw attention to particular differences between the two samples. It must be remembered, however, that the stress area was only a small part of the London Borough of Islington and thus these residents are not strictly comparable with the migrants drawn from the whole Borough. Moreover, the migrants' sample was spread over a long time span, during which time some of the social characteristics of both Islington as a whole and the stress area will have changed due to redevelopment and the spread of owner-occupation. Nevertheless, where possible we have included 1971 Census data, for the London Borough of Islington, to supplement our own data, to help establish more clearly how typical the migrants are, compared to the population of Islington as a whole.

Before turning to the data, it is important to bear in mind

that they describe the end product of an extremely complicated process which, as we pointed out in Chapter 3, involves opportunities, obstacles and positive choices for movement. What this chapter is intended to establish is the extent to which opportunities existed in practice, what choices were made on the strength of them, and why.

Let us look first at the social class composition of the migrant group. In Chapters 1, 2 and 3 we made some suggestions as to why people might wish or be able to move. First, we suggested that people move from the City very largely for housing reasons, and secondly, that people who do move for housing reasons tend to be drawn from the lower socio-economic groups. Thus one would expect that a high proportion, at the very least, of migrants to New and Expanding Towns would be manual workers, and, all other things being equal, they would very probably be the least privileged manual workers—namely the unskilled. But all other things are not equal, as we pointed out in Chapter 3, because there are a number of crucial intervening factors, not least of which is the operation of the institutions (e.g. the NETS) which simultaneously encourages and discourages the movement of the most disadvantaged. In catering for the needs of industry in New and Expanding Towns, which demands largely skilled workers, the NETS also contains countervailing mechanisms that may help less skilled workers who wish to move. But the demands of employers predominate and, as a result, a relatively high proportion of migrants to New and Expanding Towns are skilled manual workers, as we showed in Chapter 3.

Table 6 I reflects this bias. Over half the heads of household from the sample who had moved over the previous five years from Islington to New and Expanding Towns were skilled manual workers, compared to just over a quarter of the residents of the Islington stress area and about one-third of the males in the Borough of Islington and the GLC in 1971 (see Chapter 5). Conversely, there was a considerably smaller proportion of employers, professional and non-manual workers among those who had moved recently from Islington (12.9 per cent) compared to those living in the stress area (26.3 per cent) or the Borough of Islington and the GLC. Apart from confirming the conventional view of a bias among migrants towards the skilled working class, our data also show that this socio-economic composition is different from the socio-economic composition in their area of origin.

Table 6 I

Socio-economic Group* (percentages)

SEG	Islington stress area residents (1972)	New Town migrants from Islington (1972)
Employer/professional (1, 2, 3, 4, 13)	3.3	2.9
Non-manual (5, 6)	23.3	10.0
Personal service/semi-skilled (7, 10, 15)	27.4	22.9
Foremen, skilled manual and own account (8, 9, 12, 14)	27.6	58.8
Unskilled manual (11)	16.5	4.1
Armed Forces/inadequately described (16, 17)	2.1	1.2
Total	100 (512)	100 (201)

* SEG of Heads of Household
Sources: Stress Area Survey, migrants' survey

Age is the second significant variable. Were the Islington migrants younger, on the whole, than the residents of the area they left behind? Table 6 II introduces comparable data of age of heads of household: it establishes that the age profile of

Table 6 II

Age of Heads of Households (percentages)

Age	Islington stress area residents (1972)	Islington migrants at time of moving
0–4	—	—
5–15	—	—
16–25	8.8	21.9
26–35	18.2	30.4
36–45	16.4	18.0
46–55	18.4	10.5
56–65	26.2	11.5
66+	12.1	8.0
Total	100 (512)	100 (201)

Sources: Stress Area Survey, migrants' survey

migrants tends to be younger than the age profile of Islington stress area residents.

Moreover, migrants from Islington, and migrants to six New Towns in 1969 (see Table 3 II) were more similar to each other than they were to residents, either of Islington or Greater London as a whole. Thus the Islington migrants—in terms of age as in social class—appear to be *migrants* as a type, rather than Islington stress area residents, as a type. But the figures also show quite clearly that it is wrong to assume all migrants are young. The proportion of heads of household aged 36–45 are very similar for migrants and residents, and while the older groups are under-represented among the migrants, they are by no means a small percentage of all migrants. Moreover, in the oldest age group (over 65), the Islington migrants were represented in fairly similar proportion to their proportion in the stress area.

These age differences between migrants and residents are also clear when we analyse the two groups by a combination of house-hold type and age. Table 6 III uses a self-explanatory house-hold type breakdown (explained further in Appendix 2) to compare Islington migrants and residents.

Table 6 III

Household Type of Islington Migrants and Residents (percentages)

Household type	Islington migrants (at time of moving)	Islington stress area residents
1 adult alone under 65	3.5	19.1
1 adult alone over 65	3.0	6.3
2 adults alone under 45	10.0	7.6
2 adults alone 45–65	8.6	13.9
2 adults alone over 65	2.5	3.9
Related adults, no children	1.0	3.7
Young families	55.2	23.0
Older families	9.0	9.2
Non-family groups	0.0	2.7
Others	7.5	9.5
Total	100 (201)	100 (512)

The Table makes the point quite explicitly: over half of Islington migrants were young families compared to about one-quarter of Islington residents; single adults, particularly those under 65, were under-represented amongst the migrants and, to a lesser extent, adults aged 45–65 without children. Once again, it is clear that New and Expanding Towns are very successful in attracting the young skilled worker with small children.

In Chapter 3 we suggested that a major push factor for many families to move away from the Inner City might be their housing need. Table 6 IV describes three important amenities which the Islington migrants had (or did not have) in their Islington home before they moved, and which the Islington stress area residents had in 1972.

Table 6 IV
Amenities in Islington (percentages)

	London Borough of Islington 1971	Islington Stress Area Residents 1972	Islington Migrants
Fixed bath/shower			
Exclusive	56.4	48.1	41.3
Shared	22.7	32.7	25.4
None	20.9	19.2	33.3
Inside WC			
Exclusive	63.3	52.8	42.8
Shared	27.7	39.7	39.8
None	9.0	7.3	17.0
Kitchen			
Exclusive	N/A	90.7	79.1
Shared	N/A	3.6	6.0
None	N/A	5.7	14.9

Sources: Census data, 1971, Stress Area Survey, migrants' survey

This Table shows how badly the housing of the migrants—in terms of amenities—compared with that of other Islington residents both in the study area and in the Borough as a whole. While the stress area contained concentrations of bad housing conditions and, in particular, overcrowding (see page 87), the migrants, as a group of people, had originally had even worse housing conditions, except in terms of overcrowding.

Table 6 V compares occupancy rates of the Islington migrants and the stress area residents. This Table effectively reverses the position described in Table IV. The Islington stress area residents were far more overcrowded than the migrants had been before they moved. Over one-quarter of the stress area residents were living at more than 1.5 persons per room compared with 8.5 per cent of the migrants, while over one-quarter of the migrants had been living at less than half a person per room, compared with only 10 per cent of the residents.

Table 6 V
Occupancy Rates in Islington (percentages)

Persons per room*	Islington Migrants	Islington stress area residents
Below 0.5	26.9	10.2
0.5–1.0	56.2	46.8
1.1–1.5	8.5	16.7
Over 1.5	8.5	26.4
Total	100 (201)	100 (512)

*Kitchens were not included as rooms
Sources: Stress Area Survey, migrants' survey

So we have a picture of migrants moving from ill-equipped houses where they had enough space, and Islington residents grossly overcrowded, while enjoying rather better amenities. This fits the picture provided in Chapter 5 of the 'traditional' English working class as potential migrants, despite their roots in the Inner City. This picture tends to be confirmed when we look at tenure.

Table 6 VI
Tenure in Islington (percentages)

	Borough of Islington (1971)	Islington stress area residents	Islington migrants
Owner-occupied	13.4	26.7	0.0
Renting from local authority	28.7	22.5	21.5
Renting privately			
unfurnished	37.2	32.9	64.2
furnished	19.2	15.5	9.0
Tied to employment	1.4	2.2	2.0
Other		0.6	3.5
Total	100	100 (512)	100 (201)

Sources: Census data, 1971, Stress Area Survey, migrants' survey

There are three important points to be taken from the breakdown in Table VI. First, the migrants were drawn disproportionately from the unfurnished rented sector—nearly two-thirds of them had come from this relatively secure tenure category, compared to one-third of the stress area residents and just over one-third of Islington residents as a whole. This confirms the view that the migrants were actually of longer standing in the Borough of Islington than the residents of the stress area. Unfurnished lettings have, until 1974, been at a premium in Inner City areas because of their greater security than furnished lettings under the Rent Acts and have generally become less and less easy to obtain since the passage of the 1965 Act. People who have gained access to this tenure are therefore relatively privileged; they either lived in the area at a time when un-furnished lettings were more generally available or have had good enough contacts within the area to hear of such lettings becoming vacant. By contrast, the push to owner-occupation in this group, which is an alternative which also provides security, at a price, was not so great. In fact, *none* of the migrants had been owner-occupiers before they moved, com-pared to one-quarter of the stress area residents and 13.4 per cent of all the residents of the Borough of Islington in 1971.

As we suggested in the previous chapter, the quarter of the stress area residents who had managed to become owner-occupiers have a substantial stake in their present area of resi-dence. Not that this group was living in luxury accommodation, as we showed. But one can reasonably postulate that the greater financial stake of these owner-occupiers in their housing, coupled with the high value placed on owner-occupation *per se* would make this group reluctant to move, particularly if it involved a change to Development Corporation or Commission rented accommodation as a move to a New Town would probably do.

The third point of interest in Table 6 VI is the broadly similar proportions of council tenants among the migrants, the stress area residents and the Borough of Islington as a whole. These council tenants who moved had been relatively well housed in Islington—over 80 per cent of them had had exclusive use of inside lavatories, baths and kitchens and only 8 per cent of them had had exceptionally high occupancy rates. We can therefore assume that, in the main, they were occupying purpose-built local authority dwellings—the kind that families on Islington Borough Council's housing waiting list are currently queueing up to obtain. Thus, this group of council tenants who moved is a rather mysterious group—they were not in housing need in Islington and yet representative proportions of them were prepared to move many miles to New or Expanding Towns. When we come to look at the reasons people gave for moving, we shall get a clearer picture of the motivation of this group, but in the meantime, we can suggest that they may have been people who were rejecting aspects of Islington life generally which they disliked rather than specific drawbacks in their accommodation.

The broad picture of Islington migrants that has emerged is very similar to the 'traditional' groups discussed in Chapter 1. Indeed, the data are beginning to confirm the suggestions made by Michael Mann [1] that the traditional groups may be the very groups who now wish to leave the inner parts of conurbations that are subject to particular kinds of stress. But, given the very high proportion of unfurnished and local authority tenants among the migrants, it seems as though some substantial explanation will have to be found for the voluntary movement of the very people who could otherwise be expected to have deep roots in the local 'community'.

In order to elucidate this mystery, let us examine the length of residence and links with family and friends for both the migrants and the residents of the stress area. This should tell us more about how relatively 'rooted' the migrants were before they left Islington. The next Table 6 (VII) gives the length of

Table 6 VII
Length of Residence in the Borough of Islington of Migrant Heads of Household (percentages)

Length of residence	Migrant heads of household
1 year or less	1.5
Over 1 year up to 2 years	5.0
2 years to 5 years	10.5
5 years to 10 years	13.0
10 years to 15 years	8.5
15 years to 20 years	6.0
Over 20 years	17.0
Born there	38.4
Don't know	0.5
Total	100 (201)

Source: Migrants' survey

residence in Islington of the migrant heads of household, and shows that a high proportion of them were indeed residents of very long standing. Nearly two-thirds of the migrant heads of households had either been born in the Borough or lived there more than fifteen years. An even more striking picture emerges if we look at the wives (or husbands, as the case may be) of the migrant heads of household—64 per cent of them had lived in Islington before they had married and 61 per cent of these were Islington-born.

Another way of putting the same question is to examine the place of birth of the migrant and stress area heads of household together. Table 6 VIII shows that the migrant heads of household were more likely to have been born in Islington than the residents of the stress area and that, overall, they were far more likely to have been born in the UK.

Only 12 per cent of the migrants had been born outside the

Table 6 VIII

Place of birth of migrants and stress area heads of household (percentages)

Place of birth	Islington migrants	Islington stress area residents
Islington	48.3*	26.2
Elsewhere in London	19.9	19.8
Elsewhere in UK	19.9	17.6
Total	88.1	63.6
Eire	4.5	11.9
Greece/Cyprus	0.5	5.3
Caribbean	3.0	7.0
India/Pakistan	2.0	1.8
Elsewhere outside UK	2.0	10.3
Total	100 (201)	100 (512)

* There is a serious disparity here between Tables 6 VII and 6 VIII. There is a 10 per cent difference between the numbers who claimed—in answer to two separate questions—to have been born in the area of the London Borough of Islington. There may have been some confusion, in the minds of the residents, about what areas constituted this new London Borough, which would explain this rather large difference. If this is so, then it is probably safe to assume that 48.3 per cent of the heads of household were born in Islington or its immediate surroundings.

Sources: Stress Area Survey, migrants' survey

UK compared to nearly 40 per cent of the stress area residents. And, just as significantly, only one-quarter of the stress area residents had actually been born in the area of the London Borough of Islington. But it would be quite wrong to jump to the conclusion that the stress area now houses only the foreign-born and that the native Islington and British-born are leaving *en bloc*. In fact, nearly two-thirds of the inhabitants of the stress area were born somewhere in the United Kingdom.

And if there was any kind of foreign concentration in the stress area, it was of foreigners of a very disparate kind drawn from a range of countries from white Eire (the largest group) to the black Caribbean (the second largest group). Nevertheless, if the process of migration out of London continues to attract people born in Islington disproportionately and to under-represent foreigners, then we must expect an increasing concentration of the overseas-born in Islington.

As we examine the data, we are steadily building up a picture of the 'traditional' residents of Islington moving out of their borough of origin and this, as we have pointed out already, is in line with the tentative hypothesis that the lack of desire to move out among the traditional working-class community is beginning to break down. Let us now look at links with relatives, comparing the migrants and the stress area residents. Table 6 IX shows what proportion of stress area residents and migrant heads of household had relatives of various kinds living in separate households in Islington at the time they themselves were living there. It also indicates frequency of contact.

Table 6 IX does show that the migrants did have proportionately more relatives living in Islington than the stress area residents. This was particularly true of parents and parents-in-law but this may be partially explained by differences in the ages of the two groups and the fact that the migrants, being younger, were more likely to have parents still living. But, without making comparisons, it clearly is significant that over half of the migrants had left parents living locally behind when they moved—once more, confirmation that a high proportion of the migrants were families that had been very much rooted in Islington. A very similar proportion of the migrants had had brothers and sisters and in-laws living in Islington.

If we look at frequency of contact with these relatives, we can see that the migrants claimed much more frequent contact when they were living in Islington, than the stress area residents were claiming currently.

Table 6 IX

Frequency of contact with relatives living in Islington (percentages)

| | Islington migrants | | Islington stress area residents | |
	Had this relative living in Islington	% of those who had this relative and saw him/her once a week or more	Had this relative living in Islington	% of those who had this relative and saw him/her once a week or more
Children	5.5 (11)	100 (11)	8.8 (45)	91.0 (41)
Siblings and siblings-in-law	54.7 (110)	76.4 (84)	37.7 (193)	21.2 (41)
Parents and parents-in-law	55.7 (112)	95.5 (107)	12.9 (66)	77.3 (51)

Sources: Stress Area Survey, migrants' survey

This high rate of contact may be an exaggeration—possibly a nostalgic view of the nature of past Islington ways, so it would be better to rely on the more 'factual' evidence of the actual existence of relatives in the Borough than on memories of frequent contact with them. Nevertheless, the evidence in this Table is of very great importance because it disposes of any preconceived notions that a 'sense of community' and 'roots' in a neighbourhood (as symbolized by relatives living in the same area) may be decisive factors in determining who stays and who moves. It is usually suggested that those with 'roots' of this kind are the most reluctant to move long distances, but these findings suggest that if the opportunities arise, they may not be deterred by the fact that the move would involve loosening these ties.

Our data on membership of clubs and associations do not add very much to this picture; but they do show that the migrants were much more likely to have been members of a trade union when they were living in Islington. Again, this small piece of evidence tends to confirm the picture of the 'traditional' British worker moving out of Islington.

To sum up, the picture that emerges of the migrants is of predominantly young, skilled workers living either in obsolete rented accommodation or as council tenants. In terms of ethnic group, they were disproportionately British-born compared to the sample of stress area residents and, also compared to that sample, had had far more relatives living within the area with whom they apparently maintained good contact. On the whole, the migrants' housing was extremely bad in terms of amenities but adequate in terms of space standards and good for security of tenure. Nevertheless, these families had moved far afield, effectively abandoning their predominantly older relatives in favour of better standards of accommodation elsewhere.

Is there anything in the attitudes they expressed either about Islington in general or about their own circumstances while living in the Borough that might help to explain their decision to move?

Attitudes of the Migrants to Life in Islington

The neighbourhood

The first set of Tables shows the attitudes people professed to have to the area in which they lived at the time of moving. First of all, we asked how satisfied people were with the area:

Table 6 X

Degree of satisfaction with local area (Islington)

	%
Very satisfied	18.0
Fairly satisfied	42.3
Rather dissatisfied	14.5
Very dissatisfied	22.4
DK/NA	3.0
Total	100 (201)

Source: Migrants' survey

Table 6 XI

Likes about the area (Islington)

Item	% of respondents who mentioned each aspect
Good shops	41.3
Near to relatives	30.9
Good public transport	24.9
Good for entertainment	20.4
'Roots there'	16.5
Nothing	14.0
Convenient for parks	13.5
Work was available	13.5
Central position	13.0
Pleasant area	9.0
Other	8.5
Total	205.5

Source: Migrants' survey

Clearly, many more people were very or fairly satisfied than the reverse. In order to fill in the picture, we then asked what people liked and disliked about their areas, and Tables 6 XI and 6 XII rank their likes and dislikes respectively. Each aspect that respondents mentioned was coded, which explains why each Table adds up to much more than 100 per cent. (It is clear from the total percentage, particularly in Table 6 XI, that on the whole respondents mentioned two items.)

While different physical factors were mentioned more often than 'social' factors such as 'near to relatives', the factor of living near relatives in Islington was important to nearly a third of the sample. However, the presence of the amenities of urban

Table 6 XII
Dislikes about the surrounding area (Islington)

Item	% of respondents who mentioned this aspect
Nothing	27.4
Area depressing	22.4
Area/streets dirty	21.9
Foreigners	15.0
Coloured people moving in	14.0
Disadvantages for children	14.0
Too much traffic	13.5
Area too tough	10.5
Other	10.0
Area too crowded	9.0
Area getting noisy	5.5
Everything	1.0
Poor schools	1.0
Total	165.2

Source: Migrants' survey

life—such as the shops that living near a city centre provides and entertainment facilities—and easy access to them—were obviously at the top of the respondents' minds—perhaps because the task of thinking back led to a juxtaposition of their old and new neighbourhoods and the shops of Islington may have compared particularly favourably with the shops in their New or Expanding Town.

On the whole, people appear from the evidence of Tables 6 XI and 6 XII to have had positive views about Islington—which confirms the figures about satisfaction. The highest number of respondents (27.4 per cent) said there was 'nothing' they disliked. However, two significant causes of discontent emerged. The first could be termed 'environmental': complaints about the area being dirty or depressing, becoming noisy or clogged with traffic, all attracted a significant number of mentions. Second were the number of mentions of 'foreigners' and 'coloured people' which both rank fairly high on the list, although they were mentioned by only 15 per cent or 14 per cent of the respondents respectively. When we went on to ask people whether they thought their area had been changing in any way—a question which has sometimes been used to establish a link between resentment about physical change and the arrival of newcomers—three-quarters said that it had, half of these mentioned rebuilding, a quarter said that the area was going down in social terms (as opposed to physical demolition), 21 per cent mentioned foreigners and 17 per cent mentioned coloured people. So, obviously 'change' was perceived by many; but the reference was made more to change in the physical than the social fabric.

The accommodation

Table 6 XIII shows that people had been more dissatisfied with their accommodation in Islington than with the area.

Table 6 XIII
Satisfaction with Islington accommodation

	%
Very satisfied	13.0
Fairly satisfied	34.4
Rather dissatisfied	19.0
Very dissatisfied	33.9
DK/NA	0.0
Total	100 (201)

Source: Migrants' survey

Over half the migrants said they had been dissatisfied in some sense with their accommodation: and a third said they had been very dissatisfied with it. This contrasts with just over one-third who had said that they were dissatisfied with the area, and just over 20 per cent very dissatisfied. Table 6 XIV lists in rank order the factors which respondents mentioned that they had disliked about their accommodation. As can be seen, poor facilities were mentioned by more respondents than space standards—although lack of room comes a fairly close second. This was to be expected in the light of the housing conditions described above. However, aspects of housing linked closely to age and bad management—such as disrepair—were also mentioned fairly often, compared to other aspects, thereby confirming that these respondents had been living in obsolete rather than overcrowded housing.

Table 6 XIV
Dislikes about Islington accommodation

Item	% of respondents who mentioned this aspect
Poor facilities	39.3
Other	29.9
Not enough room/no spare room	26.4
Shared facilities	19.9
Damp/leaking roof	19.9
Very old/in bad repair/uneven floors	17.5
No privacy/independence/freedom	11.5
Complaints about neighbours, 'niggers'/ prostitutes/alcoholics/vandals	10.5
Infested with rats/bugs	10.5
Too many stairs/on top floor	9.0
Nothing	8.5
Complaints about landlords: repairs not done/too many restrictions	5.5
Everything	2.0
Total	210.4

Source: Migrants' survey

Finally, let us turn to the reasons the respondents themselves gave for moving. Were these dominated—as we would expect from our evidence about their housing conditions—by a desire to obtain a better house, complete with the five standard amenities and in good repair? Or were there other reasons which were to do with social factors—a question we shall deal with in more detail later? Table 6 XV shows the reasons people mentioned initially, in rank order, together with the single reason the respondents mentioned as the most important. The Table clearly indicates that the standard of accommodation in New and Expanding Towns was the single most important factor.

Table 6 XV

Reasons for moving

Reason	% of respondents mentioning this aspect	% of respondents who said this was the most important reason for moving
Wanted better house	44.8	34.9
Other reasons	22.9	5.0
Wanted to be near relatives/ friends	21.9	9.0
Wanted to be out of London/ be in country	21.9	8.5
Other reasons connected with family, e.g. space for children to play, better schools	18.5	6.5
Were offered house by council/no chance of obtaining property in London	18.0	10.5
Health reasons/better for children's health	16.0	8.0
Job came up	15.5	6.0
Change of house and job	8.5	4.5
Firm moved here	7.5	3.5
Wanted to escape existing conditions/better ourselves	7.5	4.0
Total	203.0	100 (201)

Source: Migrants' survey

Nearly half our respondents mentioned the house as a reason for moving, and just over a third said it was the most important reason. However, in terms of the number of mentions (although not in terms of being the most important reasons) the wish to be near relatives and friends, environmental factors that affected children and health in particular were also important (over 20 per cent mentioned that they wished to be near their relatives and friends). When we look at the single most important reason given, it is perhaps significant that lack of opportunity for better housing, as represented by the answer 'we couldn't get anywhere in London' shifts into the second most important reason, albeit a long way behind the desire for a better house—though the two can obviously be linked.

Overall, the reasons distilled here suggest that the positive attraction of life in a New or Expanding Town, in terms of accommodation and environmental facilities, was the strongest factor of all in producing the decision to move. While the wish to be 'out of London' generally may have been a reflection of particular dissatisfaction with Islington, it is important to remember that a majority of the respondents found Islington a very or fairly satisfactory place to live. Or, to put it in the language of migration studies, pull was stronger than push.

Conclusions

What generalizations can be drawn out from these data about migration, in particular the attitudes of migrants to New and Expanding Towns? Using some of the hypotheses suggested in Chapters 1, 2 and 3, there are a number of points that can be made. First of all, the suggestion made in Chapter 3 that working-class people in a housing shortage might be prepared to move long distances in order to improve their housing is amply confirmed by this evidence; again and again respondents said that they had moved in order to better their housing conditions. In comparison, the question of bettering employment hardly arose. The surprising finding is about the kind of people who were moving to New and Expanding Towns. Despite the poor housing conditions in which many of them were living, they appear to have been the kinds of people who might well have been expected to stay in an area because of long familiarity and the fact that many of their friends and, in particular, relatives, continued to live there. However, our evidence suggests the contrary: people long established in an area moving away from it.

What persuaded those Inner City residents to move, apart from adverse housing conditions? There is no doubt that better opportunities for their children were of importance. Even though this aspect did not figure very largely amongst the reasons respondents gave for moving (Table 6 XV), it came into prominence, as we shall see later, when our respondents referred to the benefits they had gained from their move.

Another possible motivation for moving was referred to in Chapter 1—Josephine Klein's suggestion that 'respectables' can be divided into two sub-groups, 'status dissenters' who are aspirant, and 'traditionals' who wish not to better standards but to maintain long-standing traditional standards. In this context, the fact that three-quarters of respondents thought that Islington was 'changing' when they left it is of great significance. More-over, it was no longer true that all their friends and relatives lived in Islington—a substantial minority mentioned as a reason for moving that they wished to join friends and relatives in the New or Expanding Town.

Indeed, we have evidence of a quite substantial element of chain migration. No less than 70 per cent of the migrants said they had known someone living in the New or Expanding Town before they themselves moved to one. As far as friends and relatives living in their present town were concerned, nearly half this group had had relatives living in the same town before the migrants themselves moved, and 17 per cent of this group had had friends living in the same town. We also asked respondents whether there was anyone now living in the same town who had known them before moving there. A substantial minority of respondents identified such people; and 70 per cent of this group came from Islington, and only four families from outside London. Nearly half the respondents who answered this question said that these people had come specifically because the respondents themselves were already living there, the majority of them being relatives.

Thus one can argue that for many of the respondents, Islington was no longer the centre of their social world since its focus—in terms of social and kinship networks—had shifted elsewhere, and the look of it, both physically and socially, was changing beyond recognition. Change in Islington and its increasing heterogeneity in terms of ethnic and social class appears to have become a 'push' factor in the migration process, just as the very homogeneity of the New and Expanding Town was a 'pull' factor. However, the data do not point very strongly to this factor as a main motivation to move, although it is diffi-cult not to assume that some factor like a 'flight to the suburbs' was in fact helping to push people out—in particular, this would help to explain the departure of the council tenants who were well housed in Islington. This is a subject worth investigating further, since it is likely that the general satisfaction that the migrants had with their new accommodation and environment (explored in Chapter 8) was actually masking the 'push' factors which had been at work at the time they moved. Hence the reasons this sample gave for moving may over-emphasize the positive factors in the New and Expanding Towns, which they had discovered since they had moved. (It will become clear later that the New and Expanding Towns did provide an attractive social environment; this may be partly because people have found more of their 'own kind' in the new location.)

But before turning away from the topic of the motivation of the group that actually moved out, it is worth looking at the other side of the coin and ask why the people in the stress area stayed there. Was it because they were not aware of opportunities to move out? Alternatively, did they choose to stay, despite knowing that they could move away? It is only when these questions are also answered that we can fully distinguish those factors that 'push' and 'pull' people about the map and that can be changed by policy-makers and social engineers.

Reference

1. MANN, MICHAEL, op. cit.

Chapter Seven

Knowledge and Opinions about Moving

As we pointed out in Chapter 3, knowledge of opportunities to move away either to better jobs or to better housing is a key element in the process of moving. Many government reports, in particular the Cullingworth report [1] on the allocation of council housing and the Seebohm report [2] have pointed out the crucial importance of information in other social problem areas.

When we asked the sample of migrants how they had first heard of the possibility of moving to a New or Expanding Town, by far the highest proportion (two-fifths) had said they had heard through a friend, and 15 per cent had heard through the firm for which either the husband or wife worked. Information from official sources, such as Employment Exchanges or Borough housing departments, had initially permeated through to only under half the sample. Eighteen per cent had heard through an Employment Exchange, 9.5 per cent when they had put their name down on the Borough housing list, 8.0 per cent through a letter from the GLC and 5 per cent through an advertisement in a newspaper. Thus informal networks of information are of paramount importance, and this, in itself, may restrict information to a particular class of person, especially those who have friends and relatives who have already moved to a New or Expanding Town.

In the previous chapter, we noted what appeared to be a considerable amount of chain migration. Those who already have

friends and relatives in a New or Expanding Town might
therefore have two 'extra' reasons for moving to one themselves:
first, they know about these opportunities for movement and,
second, since friends or family have already made the move
neither does it seem an unusual or disturbing thing to do, nor, if
these friends live in the same town, are social contacts severed.
Rather, such contacts can be cemented. It may be that the
migrants were originally 'privileged' in this sense, compared to
the stress area residents, and we have data that help us to begin
to test this proposition. For example, the stress area residents
were asked the following question: 'Some people have left the
Islington area over the last 10 years to move to New Towns.
Have you ever visited a New Town outside London?' Just over
half the stress area residents replied that they had. In comparison,
the migrants were asked, first of all, about people whom
they knew before they moved who had been living in a New
or Expanding Town, and a high proportion (over two-thirds)
had said they had known such people. In answer to the question
'Before you moved, did you ever visit these friends or relatives
in the New or Expanding Town they lived in?' over half (57
per cent) said 'Yes'. Visiting friends and relatives is a rather
more specific activity than just 'visiting' a New or Expanding
Town and so one must assume that while the difference between
the stress area residents and the migrants is not great, it is
possible that a slightly higher proportion of migrants had 'visited'
than of the stress area residents. But it is when we turn to
breakdowns of the stress area sample that it becomes clear that
some groups were far more likely to have been to a New or
Expanding town than others. Table 7 I shows the proportions
of particular groups of people who said they had paid such a
visit and shows that those groups who are usually the least
'privileged' in terms of income and housing were the least likely
to have done so. For example, only one-third of the West Indians
had paid such visits compared to over two-thirds of the families
with heads of household born in Inner London, and over half
of the families where the head came from other parts of Britain.
Only 7.5 per cent of the Greek Cypriots had been to a New
or Expanding Town. A similar pattern reveals itself when we
look at tenure: only one-third of furnished tenants had been,
compared with well over a half of both local authority and
private unfurnished tenants. While there were not such great

Table 7 I
Proportion of stress area residents who had visited New and Expanding Towns by place of birth, tenure, length of residence, and socio-economic group

	Had visited %
Place of birth of head of household:	
Inner London	67.5
Rest of GB	58.3
Eire	47.6
West Indies	33.4
Greece/Cyprus	7.5
Elsewhere	22.6
Tenure in Islington:	
Owner-occupier	44.9
Council tenant	60.0
Private furnished	34.2
Private unfurnished	59.0
Other	50.0
Length of residence in accommodation:	
Less than 1 year	44.6
1–5 years	51.6
5–10 years	48.2
10+ years	55.8
SEG:	
Manager/professional	50.0
Non-manual	58.5
Personal service/semi-skilled	48.2
Foreman/skilled manual	58.8
Unskilled manual	43.8
Total sample	51.4

Source: Stress Area Survey

differences between the socio-economic groups, it is still important to note that under half the unskilled and semi-skilled workers had visited New and Expanding Towns compared with well over half of the non-manual and skilled manual workers. Here we have clear evidence that visiting the Towns was an activity that the more 'privileged' were more likely to have undertaken, thereby obtaining the insights necessary for an informed decision to move. These opportunities to form one's own opinion and make a decision to act on that opinion were restricted goods.

But before turning to the opinions which these visitors had

formed of the New and Expanding Towns, there are two more important pieces of data from the stress area survey which throw some light on the knowledge that these respondents had of the procedures of getting to a New Town and their perception of their eligibility for one. The stress area sample were asked to agree or disagree with a number of statements, two of which referred specifically to movement there. The first statement—'I wouldn't be able to move to a New Town unless I had a job there first'—was really to test knowledge of procedures of movement and although it is not *strictly* true because people can buy houses in a New Town or rent privately without first having jobs there, it is generally true that the people contained within this sample almost certainly needed a job before they could be eligible for New Town Commission or Development Corporation housing. In fact, only 42 per cent of the sample 'strongly agreed' with this statement, and a high proportion (33 per cent) were clearly uncertain because they said they neither agreed nor disagreed—and one must assume that most of these actually said that they did not know. Interestingly, however, when one looks at these data broken down by place of birth, tenure and SEG, it was the West Indians who displayed the highest accuracy since 61 per cent of them said they 'strongly agreed' with the statement. Apart from this group, there were rather small variations of opinion between the different groups, except that management and non-manual SEGs were rather more likely to disagree strongly. These data reveal that a high proportion of respondents were very vague about the whole subject of movement to New or Expanding Towns and had probably never thought about it before.

The second statement was: 'People like me would never be eligible for New Town housing.' There are, of course, some problems with the statement. The word 'eligible' is probably a difficult word for many respondents to understand, and, furthermore, it is impossible to know what the respondents had in mind when they thought of people 'like me'. Did they identify themselves as foreigners, Englishmen, black, white, skilled, unskilled, men, women, workers, pensioners, working class, middle class? It is also impossible to tell what the word 'never' meant in this context, because one can presumably think one may not be currently eligible, but might become so in the future.

Nevertheless, the results are worth quoting here because they give some idea of those who would never consider a move to a New or Expanding Town. A very high proportion of the whole sample—38 per cent—strongly agreed that they would *never* be eligible for New Towns housing. And this high proportion runs consistently when the sample is broken down by class, tenure and birthplace. The groups who show the highest certainty that they are not eligible are those born in Inner London, the Greek Cypriots and the unskilled manual workers. The groups showing the highest level of disagreement about their eligibility (thereby presumably asserting it) were the West Indians and the managerial and professional group. Taken together, these pieces of evidence imply strong feelings of lack of opportunity and also ignorance, which are common to many different groups. Moreover, it is clear that lack of knowledge and hazy or wrong perceptions constitute a major 'intervening obstacle' since they affect at least a third of the stress area residents.

Reactions to New Towns

Clearly, a crucial item of information is the reaction of those who had actually seen New Towns. For while a major obstacle to movement may be lack of knowledge, no amount of additional information is going to persuade people who do not like the idea of living in a New or Expanding Town to move to one. We asked the 253 stress area residents who had at some time visited a New or Expanding Town to say what they thought of them. First, we asked them 'What do you think it is like to live in a New Town?' Table 7 II shows the answers they gave and indicates that these respondents, nearly half of whom thought the New Towns were 'quite pleasant' and only 17 per cent of whom thought they were 'very pleasant' were rather luke-warm in their response. In contrast, the migrants seemed to have had very positive views about New and Expanding Towns for a long time, since when we asked those who had friends and relatives living there what they thought it was like to live there (before they moved to one), nearly two-thirds said they had thought it 'very pleasant'. This backward glance at their opinions was probably highly coloured by their own satisfactory experience in a New or Expanding Town since that time, but the startling contrasts between the two responses probably bear some relation to reality.

But Table 7 III shows that the stress area residents were really very negative indeed about their own position vis-à-vis New Towns. The 'visitors' were asked if they thought they personally would move to a New Town if they had the opportunity. Over a third were very positive they would not and an additional 30 per cent thought they probably would not.

Table 7 II

Stress area residents' and migrants' original views of life in New and Expanding Towns

	Stress area residents %	Migrants %
Very pleasant	17.0	61.4
Quite pleasant	47.0	28.1
Not very pleasant	18.2	4.4
Not at all pleasant	12.3	1.8
Don't know	5.5	4.4
Total	100 (253)	100 (201)

Sources: Stress Area Survey, migrants' survey

Table 7 III

Stress area residents' attitudes to moving to New Towns

Opinion	%
Yes, we would definitely move	15.8
Yes, we would probably move	21.3
No, we don't think we would move	20.6
No, we definitely would not move	37.5
Don't know	4.7
Total	100 (253)

Source: Stress Area Survey

Thus, we must acknowledge that many people living in Inner London simply do not like the idea of living in New or Expanding Towns themselves, and that is a very good reason for not wishing to move to one. Unfortunately, due to a coding error, we cannot give the distribution of reasons why people preferred not to move to a New or Expanding Town. However, we can list the coded reasons, taken from answers to the open-ended question 'What are your reasons for saying that?' They were:

Roots here/have lived here a long time/too old to move.
Friends are here/too difficult to make new friends/prefer to
be with people I know.
Used to London/prefer it here/couldn't settle elsewhere/would
be a stranger.
New Town soul-less/lacks character/unfriendly.
Lack of amenities/poor shopping facilities/lack of entertain-
ment/transport, etc.
Too far from work/don't want to change jobs/prospects and
wages better in London/other difficulties connected with work.
Could not leave aged relative, prefer to live near family.
Other reasons connected with family.
Criticisms of planning.
Other reasons.

As can be seen, most of the coded up answers refer to the
familiarity of London and Islington, and the proximity of friends
and family in their present area. Thus, on balance, people who
had seen them did not really like New and Expanding Towns
and they found compensations in Islington for the bad housing
many of them occupied.

But before deciding that the residents of Islington stress area
lived there because they preferred it to anywhere else—which
the previous paragraph might imply—it is important to remember both the lack of information, and the lack of income and
general opportunities to better oneself that were stressed earlier
in this report. It is also worth looking closely at another piece
of data that applies to the whole sample, rather than just to
the 'visitors' to the New or Expanding Town. The whole sample
was asked to agree or disagree with the statement 'I would never
want to leave this area, even if I got better accommodation
elsewhere.' Only 28 per cent of the total sample strongly agreed
with this statement compared with 41 per cent who strongly
disagreed. Thus great attachment to the area really does not
seem to have affected the majority of these residents—although
the fact that over a quarter did feel a very strong sense of
attachment is not so small a proportion that it can be ignored.

When the sample was broken down by place of birth, tenure,
and SEG, some interesting differences emerged between the

different groups. Immigrants (except the Greek Cypriots) tended to have a slightly stronger disposition to stay in the area. Among the tenure groups, owner-occupiers and council tenants seemed less likely to wish to move, and unfurnished tenants more likely. Manual workers had considerably less disposition to leave than the professional and managerial groups. Even so, a third of both skilled and unskilled manual workers strongly disagreed with this statement thus showing that for almost as many a better house was more important than anything else to do with location. Indeed, the evidence suggests that for almost all the groups the conflict between a better house elsewhere and attachment to their current neighbourhood was sharply divisive. The only safe generalization one can make is that different people feel very strongly on both subjects.

What conclusions can be drawn from these slightly patchy data? Firstly, they indicate that the question of moving to New or Expanding Towns did not really cross most people's minds. In this connection it is interesting to note that of our sample of 117 stress area residents who said they thought they would probably move within the next two years, only five appear to have known something about a scheme to move people to New or Expanding Towns. Moreover, even when people had visited a New Town—and over half the stress area residents had —their reactions to them were rather negative. But this does not mean to say that people were overwhelmingly in favour of staying where their 'roots' were. In fact, it looks as though a high proportion of the residents were not at all attached to their local area—a conclusion supported by the evidence reported in the previous chapter.

References

1. *Council Housing: purposes, procedures and priorities*, op. cit.
2. *Report of Committee on Local Authority and Allied Personal Social Services* ('Seebohm Report') (Cmnd 3703, HMSO, 1968).

Chapter Eight

Life in the New and Expanding Towns

What was life like for the migrant group who had made the momentous decision to dig up their roots and move out? Were they leading lonely and depressing lives, lived out in isolation within the splendour of their damp-free walls? If they were, was their new accommodation adequate compensation for lack of social intercourse, or were they positively unhappy with all aspects of their new life? On the other hand, were they happy and satisfied with both their physical and social environment? Or were there added problems—for example, a rise in the cost of living largely ascribable to increases in rent—which tarnished an otherwise satisfactory life?

We tried to tackle these questions in two ways: first, by asking questions of our sample of Islington movers which might throw light on their attitudes to their new abode, and second by one of the present writers talking to a small group of people who had recently moved with one of the firms we had studied before the workers moved.

The 'small group' was, in fact, very small indeed—thirteen families in all. However, it was thought worth interviewing them because:

(a) it was possible to compare their current circumstances with their previous position in London;

(b) it was possible to interview them as families and the researcher welcomed the chance to talk to people in a completely 'open' situation; and

(c) most important, in almost all families the chief wage earner

was an unskilled manual worker and thus fell into the
category of a 'disadvantaged group'.

This last point meant that our very small sample of unskilled workers in the major migrant survey—only seven in
all—would be usefully supplemented by these interviews and
also that particular insights could be gained about the problems
of low-wage earners in New and Expanding Towns since the
basic wage for workers in this firm was £23.00 and there was
little or no overtime.

Attitudes to Life in the New and Expanding Towns

The overwhelming feeling that came over in both surveys was
of general satisfaction. Indeed, some of the respondents in the
small survey were positively euphoric. As one elderly respondent
put it:

> This is like paradise to us. It's as near to it we've ever been and
> are ever likely to get!

When we asked the respondents in the major survey, 'Taking
everything into account, do you think you made the right decision to move?', 87 per cent said they thought they had made
the right decision, 12 per cent thought they had made the wrong
decision, and 1 per cent were undecided. Thus there had been
very few errors, although, as was clear from the small survey,
if a family thought they had mistakenly made the initial move,
the difficulties of getting accommodation back in their old area
were such that it was almost better to stay where they were.
    Tables 8 I and 8 II show what reasons the larger sample gave
for feeling the way they did. It is clear from Table 8 I that
the house was regarded as the greatest gain, but close behind
were general gains for the children. In fact, mention of children
was very high indeed given that children's health and schooling
were mentioned as well (14.5 per cent and 12.5 per cent of
the respondents mentioned these respectively). Just under a
quarter claimed they felt 'happier' or had gained 'peace of mind'.
As can be seen from Table 8 II, of the twenty-four who said they
were unhappy with the move, half said they were generally

miserable. Fourteen respondents mentioned some aspect of their job—more often the low wages—that had caused them disquiet. It must be noted that this is a tiny proportion of the whole sample of 201, although we shall return to the question of the cost of living later.

Table 8 I

Reasons given for making the right decision to move

Reason	% of respondents who mentioned this reason
Better house here/own house	35.4
Freedom for children/good place to bring up children/children happier/space to play	29.9
Happier in ourselves/peace of mind	22.9
Other answers	21.4
Better environment/better place to live	18.0
Better for health/children's health	14.5
Schools are better/children doing well/ better prospects for children	12.5
Cleaner/fresh air	11.5
Better jobs here/happy in job	10.5
Have made friends/people are very friendly/ friendly atmosphere	6.0
More open/near coast/out of London	4.5
Have spare room/visitors can stay here	0.5
Total	187.6

Table 8 II

Reasons given for making the wrong decision to move

Reason	% of respondents who mentioned this reason
A miserable place/has unhappy memories/has caused unhappiness	6.0
Other answers	4.5
Low wages/poor pay	4.0
Scarcity of jobs/restricted choice of work	3.0
Loneliness/miss friends/relatives	1.5
Total	19.0

Since the house itself was obviously of such great importance we asked the major sample what they liked or disliked about their accommodation. First of all, two-fifths said there was nothing they disliked about it, although nearly a quarter (22 per cent) had criticisms to make about the internal design.

The smaller sample—while almost all of them were very pleased with the houses themselves—also had some telling criticisms of the internal design. For example, a family with a four-bedroomed house thought it odd that their fourth bedroom, which was intended for a very old and frail aunt, should be without a central heating outlet. As a result, the aunt had had to sleep in the dining area during the winter and during this time the family ate in the kitchen which was too small for that purpose. Others complained that back doors opened off sitting-rooms, so that the carpets got muddy. Most of these respondents also felt that there should be opportunities for them to comment on the design of their houses and estates to those responsible for planning the rest of the town. Such opportunities had not been made available to them, and this was strongly regretted.

As far as the likes about the accommodation were concerned, the highest proportion of respondents (43 per cent) mentioned the space they now had, and in particular 'room for the children'. Nearly one-third (29 per cent) of the large sample mentioned the garden—a great gain for many of the respondents, only 3 per cent of whom had previously lived in a whole house and therefore (one must assume) probably had access to at least a back yard. About a quarter mentioned specific facilities such as central heating or the kitchen. Nineteen per cent said they liked 'everything' about the place. The smaller sample also particularly stressed the extra space they had gained. Many, for the first time in their lives, found themselves able to put visitors up in a spare room. The house had suddenly become the holiday home of relatives left behind in London and, indeed, when the researcher visited families at the weekends there was much evidence of parents and parents-in-law who had come from London for a few days. The gardens were also mentioned by all the respondents. For some families, they were merely extremely useful places to hang out washing, store odds and ends, take the motor-bike to pieces or leave the children to play—a real luxury compared to the difficulty of organizing these things in London flats or rooms. But for many of them, the small patches of green were also a place to grow things—which for almost all of them, apart from the two families who had previously had a garden, was a totally new activity and took up a lot of spare time. One elderly man—one of the gardeners with previous experience—already had tomato plants climbing up the side of the house.

'New Town Blues'

One of the aspects that is frequently mentioned with reference to New Towns, particularly by the press, is the 'New Town blues'. The implication is that people find it difficult to make new friends and often the wives are described as leading bitter and isolated lives.

There are other aspects of both New and Expanding Towns which are more to do with the provision of—or lack of—local amenities. An image exists of islands of estates surrounded by mud, serviced by a bus once in a blue moon, and cheerless community centres that are regularly smashed up by teenage vandals who have nothing better to do.

But we have already seen that there seems to have been a considerable amount of chain migration, and, in particular, nearly a quarter of the respondents in the larger sample said that one of their reasons for moving was to be near friends and relatives. Thus the notion that people might be very lonely seems likely not to be a problem at all for about a quarter of the major sample. The major survey did, in fact, present a picture of contentment and good neighbour relations. However, the survey interviewed heads of household only, a very high proportion of whom (89 per cent) were men, which means that women's views —as a group—are not easily ascertained. But, if we take the men's views as representative of the whole family—which may, of course, be unfair but is the best we can do in the circumstances—then a very high proportion claimed that their new area was as 'friendly' or 'more friendly' than their old Islington area. Only a quarter said the area was less friendly. Of course, 'friendliness' is a difficult concept to grasp or describe and a belief that people are more 'friendly' may range from a feeling of greater security through to actual intercourse with many more people. So we also asked respondents: 'Do you have as many close friends here as you had in Islington, more or fewer?', and in answer to that question almost half (44 per cent) said they had fewer, but over half (55 per cent) said they had as many or more. Indeed, nearly one-third (30 per cent) said they now had more close friends.

We do have some clues about how isolated the women were. Out of 175 heads of household who were married, 78 (45 per cent) had wives who were working full or part-time. We asked these respondents whether their wives had taken up working in any way as a result of moving to the New or Expanding Town. Fifty-five respondents said the move had nothing to do with it, sixteen said it was because they needed more money as a result of the move and only seven said that their wives had wanted something to do and did not want to stay at home alone. However, these figures apply to just under half the total number of wives—unfortunately our survey tells us nothing about the other half. Nevertheless, if we take the husbands' word for it, social life seems to have been satisfactory.

The thirteen families in the small sample were in rather a different position. Only one of them—who had come through the ISS—had wanted to come specifically to Bletchley and that family had chosen that town, interestingly, because the wife's mother was already there. So for all the others, the fact that they had moved to Bletchley was purely circumstantial and nothing to do with a particular desire to be near familiar faces. On the other hand, all those who worked together knew each other and they had moved into two very small patches of the new city of Milton Keynes (see Appendix 1). Thus the basis for close friendship was already well established between most of the men, and some of the wives.

On the larger estate (see again Appendix 1), one of the 'places' was locally known by the name of the firm and while people in this 'place' tended to claim that they were increasingly branching out beyond social contacts with friends made at work, the researcher formed the opinion that social contact both within and outside the houses amongst this group of workers was still very strong. One respondent mentioned that one of the factors in his decision to move had been the comforting knowledge that there would be familiar faces around, and in practice this contact extended to the wives as well, so that wives of male workers had become very close friends. One worker claimed that one of the most satisfactory things about this new life was that, having come through the ISS, he had found his 'mates' at work and he and two other households where the men had worked at the same firm were very close indeed. Of course, these relationships can cut both ways—one respondent did say that he and his wife were initially concerned that they would all be too much in each other's pockets. But the general impression was that those who wished to keep themselves to themselves could do so, while those who needed company—so long as they were not over-dependent—could find it on their doorsteps. This proximity could also have proved a source of jealousy and gossip, but the researcher formed the impression that, apart from some chaffing amongst the men about who had still not got around to home decorating, the fact that some had refrigerators and cars was not a source of jealousy, and while all agreed that 'gossip' was 'around' if you wanted to hear it, nobody mentioned it as an unpleasant factor. The feeling seemed to be that they were all 'in the same boat'; the homogeneity of the wages within the firm obviously contributed to this, as did the recognition by all that they needed to be very careful in order to survive financially.

When we asked the major sample about their likes and dislikes in the surrounding area, 80 per cent thought their present neighbourhood better than in Islington and 45 per cent were generally very satisfied with it. Twenty-eight per cent said there was 'nothing' they disliked about their neighbourhood. However, some criticisms were made of lack of public transport and the need for a car (24 per cent) and the lack of entertainment facilities (21 per cent). Eighteen per cent mentioned poor shopping facilities or that shopping was too expensive. However, compared to the vociferous and frequent complaints about food prices that came from the smaller sample, this last percentage is surprisingly low. Every single respondent in the smaller sample complained at length about the cost of living in the New Town claiming that prices for all goods, and food in particular, were considerably higher than in London. They blamed this on the lack of choice between shops and tended to accuse the Development Corporation of not pressing hard enough to get the large chain stores to set up in their area. The complaints were difficult to verify and were, no doubt, exacerbated by the increase in rents which almost all the respondents had experienced. Cost of living is a subject we shall return to but it is worth mentioning here that for the smaller sample the shops—and lack of them—were probably a major scapegoat for a very pressing problem. Public transport was also a bone of contention in the smaller sample and was often linked to a discussion of lack of adequate shopping facilities. All the respondents found they had to go to a major city to buy goods where choice was important —e.g. children's shoes—and any journey was a heavy expense and a chore. Five families mentioned that they often used taxis. One man exclaimed that the bus company must have had shares in the local taxi firm since the one was so bad that it made the other an absolute necessity. Another young couple thought a car was such a necessity that it was a major reason why the husband had left his job with the original firm—for whom he had worked for seven years—and taken an unpleasant job where he worked sixty hours a week for £40 take-home pay. As his wife put it:

> We don't believe in H.P. We're saving to buy a car. You're stranded down here without one. When we've got it the journey to work will be easier—at the moment he has to catch the 7 a.m. bus for an 8 a.m. start. But he won't be working there for ever!

Moreover, once in the country people wanted to explore it and found it frustrating to be dependent on local buses or organized trips. Another problem which was frequently mentioned was the distance of the general hospital—ten to fifteen miles away depending where one lived. Without cars, hospital visiting was almost out of the question, and this had proved a problem for the two households where one member had been in hospital for two months and where another needed intensive out-patient care. The latter found it easier and cheaper to continue to go to a London hospital using the cheap day return rail fares than to go to the nearer, but less accessible local hospital. Nevertheless, people had managed, either by using public transport or by going out with friends who had cars, to visit a variety of local places of interest ranging from stately homes to other New Towns and major metropolitan areas. Indeed, the sharing of a car as a resource was an important element in cementing the relationships between different households. In one case an elderly single man who worked for the same firm had been adopted as a 'grandpa' to another family with children and the two households used his car together. But these sorts of arrangements are not ideal and do not solve the major problem of access to good things in the surrounding localities. Any Development Corporation or local authority, therefore, particularly one that wishes to recruit the 'poor' must take into account the need for reliable, frequent and *cheap* public transport not only within the town but beyond it.

As far as leisure pursuits were concerned, over half the major sample (56 per cent) strongly agreed with the statement 'There's not much to do here compared with Islington' and a further 22 per cent slightly agreed. But this statement tended to force people to compare the amenities of Islington with those of the New or Expanding Town and almost inevitably the latter compared badly. But it was clear from the smaller sample that leisure pursuits had changed in subtle ways. Most telling was the couple who had rented a colour television to compensate for the weekly visit to the cinema which they had had to give up since they had moved to a town with no cinema within ten miles. This family, like many of the others, was spending much more time at home. Others were doing positive things with new-found space—both inside and immediately outside the house. Gardening has already been mentioned, but one couple who had been living in two rooms in London were sleeping in the second bedroom so that they could put the billiard table in the larger bedroom. The husband in this household said:

> I don't find time to go out like I used to—the cinema and that. I go for a walk with the dog instead. Saturday is my favourite day—I love horse racing and I walk down to Fenny Stratford with the dog to put a bet on. At other times I play records. Or we go to the Bingo.

Walking was a leisure pursuit that people had adopted since they arrived, and many of them went on organized trips or shared cars to go to local sights. One elderly worker who lived by himself said whenever he went for a trip in his car—either to work or the shops—he always deliberately took the long way round so he could appreciate the countryside. Another woman said:

> I'm not moaning about the shops—I *love* walking to the shops every day.

When the same person was asked whether she ever got lonely she said:

> Sometimes—I miss the family. But there is shopping every day, the garden and that—we never even had a window box before.

The aspects of New and Expanding Town living that the major sample mentioned that they liked reflect the general appreciation of their openness and easy access to the countryside. Table 8 III lists in rank order what these respondents said they liked about their present area, and, as can be seen, the physical aspect of the town seem to be the most appreciated.

Table 8 III

Likes about present area (New or Expanding Town)

Reason	% of respondents who mentioned this aspect
Clean/quiet/nice surroundings/no industry	32.4
Open spaces/nice views	27.9
Near the country	25.4
Safe for children/good for children	24.9
Convenient for shops	15.5
Other	15.5
Neighbours friendly/nice people/no hooligans	13.5
Fresh air/healthy atmosphere	13.0
Convenient for schools/good school in area	11.0
Like gardens/trees	10.0
Well-planned estate	8.0
Convenient for transport	7.0
Central position/convenient for London	5.0
Nothing	4.5
Within reach of coast	4.5
Good health service	0.5
Near relatives	0.0
Total	218.6

Source: Migrants' survey

The 'New Town blues', if we take it to mean loneliness and a lack of things to do, seems not to have affected any but a tiny minority of the two samples. It was, however, interesting to note that when the respondents in the small sample were asked whether they knew what was meant by 'New Town blues' three of them mentioned money problems. As one man put it:

> A lot of the trouble for other people is money. And there aren't the jobs they said there would be for women.

Indeed, the cost of living was foremost in the minds of almost all the respondents in the small sample. As one older worker who was bringing home £18.40 a week said:

> When the rents go up to £10.00 and I'm paying £8.00 a week for food, who's going to pay the electric bill?

The Cost of Living

Looking at the larger sample first, it is clear from Table 8 IV that rents (which for our purposes included rates) were very much higher in the New or Expanding Town than in Islington.

Table 8 IV

Rent and Rates in Islington and the New and Expanding Towns

Rent and rates per week	% of households paying this amount	
	In Islington	In NET
Under £1.00	3.0	—
£1.00–£2.00	2.5	—
£2.00–£3.00	18.5	0.5
£3.00–£4.00	20.9	6.1
£4.00–£5.00	20.0	15.6
£5.00–£6.00	16.5	37.2
£6.00–£7.00	7.0	28.2
£7.00 plus	7.0	9.6
DK/NA	4.0	3.0
Total	100 (201)	100 (201)

Source: Migrants' survey

In Islington two-thirds of the sample had been paying less than £5.00 per week in rent and rates; in the New or Expanding Town 78 per cent were paying more than £5.00 per week. Given these rather high increases what did our respondents think about it? We asked our respondents if they had found life more expensive and over half (55 per cent) of them said that they were finding life a struggle though 41 per cent said they could afford the increases. Not surprisingly, as the following Table shows, the lower-paid socio-economic groups found it more difficult. Of course, once our sample is broken down into smaller categories the numbers become dangerously small for us to draw any conclusions, but the fact that larger proportions of semi- and unskilled workers and the unemployed found the cost of living a struggle makes sense. This obviously has serious implications for any policies the New Towns may adopt for the recruitment of the poorer 'minorities'. But there are some crumbs of comfort for those Development Corporations committed to the recruitment of the 'disadvantaged' and in difficulties about finding the revenue to cover the costs of building new dwellings. When we asked what our respondents had found more expensive, they more often mentioned items—such as food and clothing—that can only indirectly be laid at the doors of the Development Corporations and local authorities in that these

Table 8 V

Whether respondents could 'afford' new town expenses by SEG of head of household Socio-Economic Group

	Employer/ Professional		Non- manual		Personal service/ semi-skilled		Foreman/ skilled		Unskilled manual		Own account		Not Working	
	%		%		%		%		%		%		%	
We can afford it	60.0		72.8		34.5		41.6		33.4		44.5		25.0	
It's a struggle	40.0		27.3		62.1		55.4		66.7		55.6		65.0	
DK	—		—		3.4		3.0		—		—		10.0	
Total	100	(5)	100	(11)	100	(29)	100	(65)	100	(6)	100	(9)	100	(20)

Source: Migrants' survey

Table 8 VI

Items regarded as 'more expensive' than in Islington

Item	% of respondents (who thought life more expensive) mentioning this item
Food	67.9
Clothes	47.3
Travelling	42.5
Rents	32.9
Everything	21.3
Heating	7.6
Other	4.2
Total	223.7

Source: Migrants' survey

institutions could possibly be accused of not allowing enough choice in retail shops. Table 8 VI indicates what items respondents mentioned that they regarded as more expensive: as can be seen, rents were not the most frequently mentioned item, although nearly a third mentioned them.

Sixty-nine per cent of the major sample paid out between 10 per cent and 30 per cent of their take-home pay on rent and rates, but when these respondents had lived in Islington 21 per cent of them had paid out less than 10 per cent of their income, compared to only 14 per cent after moving to the New or Expanding Town.

These figures raise questions about the incomes of the residents. In the small sample, there were two families who had made spectacular sacrifices of income in order to move to a New or Expanding Town and get better accommodation. In one case, the husband and wife had had a joint take-home income in London of approximately £60.00 a week; this joint income had dropped after the move to approximately £30.00 a week. In the other case, the husband had had to give up a second, part-time job that brought in £14–£15.00 a week, and he had *volunteered* for a drop in income once he had moved because he found it impossible to manage his financial affairs when he was paid a monthly salary, and preferred a weekly wage. Thus it would seem useful to attempt to compare the wages of the respondents in the large sample with the wages of workers elsewhere.

Table 8 VII compares the head of household's take-home pay with net household income, which included pensions, family allowances and other social security payments. According to the April 1972 New Earnings Survey, average gross earnings for full-time males in the Outer Metropolitan Area were £34.8. Table 8 VII indicates that gross earnings were probably rather lower than this, but once the rest of the household's income is taken into account then nearly half (48.5 per cent) of the sample were getting net incomes of over £30.00 per week (this probably being the best net figure to compare with gross earnings of £3.00 or £4.00 more). Thus, households in the New or Expanding Town were reaching average working-class standards *so long as* other members of the household worked; and this has serious implications for the provision of work in New and Expanding Towns not just for manual male workers but for women as well. This

Table 8 VII

Head of household take-home pay and net household income

Income per week (net)	% of head of household taking this home	% of households with this net income
Under £10	—	5.0*
£10–£12	0.5	5.0*
£12–£14	0.5	2.0*
£14–£16	2.0	2.0
£16–£18	1.5	1.0
£18–£20	4.0	1.5
£20–£25	23.4	9.5
£25–£30	21.9	21.4
£30–£35	13.5	13.5
£35–£40	8.5	17.5
£40–£45	3.0	6.0
£45–£50	2.5	6.5
£50–£60	—	3.5
£60–£70	—	0.5
£70–£80	—	1.0
Head of household retired	15.5	—
Refusal	2.0	2.0
DK/NA	1.5	2.5
Total	100 (201)	100 (201)

* The reason why a higher percentage appear to have lower 'household income' than 'head-of-household income' is because of the inclusion of pensioners and pensions under 'household income'. Pensioners fell into the 'head of household retired' category in the 'head-of-household' column.

is particularly important since council house rents in district and metropolitan housing authorities are on average lower than for the brand new dwellings of the Mark II New Towns, and will probably continue to be so. Thus the higher wages paid elsewhere will put New and Expanding Town tenants at a relative disadvantage unless they can supplement their household incomes through the employment of other members of their families.

But despite the fact that the small sample, in particular, had considerable financial anxieties—one family was keen to go back to London because they found life too expensive—the interiors of almost all the houses had an overwhelming air of affluence. Two families had rented colour televisions, every house had fitted carpets in the living room. Thus the 'poverty' of these people (most of whom were paying £6–£7.00 a week on rent) was not at all visible, but masked by damp-free rooms and picture windows looking out on to well-mown lawns. But there were three important reasons, apart from the house itself, why people had achieved an apparent high level of comfort over the nine months they had lived in their new accommodation. The most important reason was that their particular firm had agreed to pay all 'reasonable' bills for new carpets and curtains. It had not been at all clear at the time of moving on what basis the 'reasonableness' was to be assessed or whether this money was to be a loan or a gift. As a result, people had submitted bills of varying amounts, all of which had been paid. Clearly this 'masking' would not have occurred if the firm had not used its discretion to make some considerable payments to its workers; and while there appear to be conventions about how firms should treat their workers there are no hard and fast rules, and indeed there was some confusion in the minds of the respondents about the status of this money and this probably sprang from the firm's use of discretion internally between its workers.

Secondly, those families that had come through the ISS had generally taken a considerable drop in income, and while they had waited for the offer of a job and a house they had saved considerable amounts of money. One of these families had bought—amongst other things—a deep freeze on the proceeds, and another family had managed to fill their house with expensive Scandinavian furniture, cash down. While they were now spending their whole income, there had been long periods when they had not: the house for these people was more than adequate compensation for a large drop in income. The third reason was that many of these workers were elderly, and over a life-time they had collected all the furniture they needed. The real struggle was for the young workers who, given a new house, wanted to have new furniture and yet at the same time they had growing numbers of dependants.

It is impossible not to conclude, however, that for the vast majority of the respondents in both the samples the move to a New or Expanding Town had been a great success. And this was despite large jumps in rent and other living expenses which over half of the major sample claimed were making the financial side of their lives a 'struggle'. Despite this, over 80 per cent of the respondents in this survey thought their move had been worthwhile—they had found a house and garden, room for their children to play, a literal breath of fresh air, and, for many, the first chance to live out family life without interference from over-close relatives, neighbours or landlords.

Chapter Nine

The Changing Policy Context

To make sense of the findings of the study so far, we shall have to move back from the particular to the general, and try to assess how far the process of planned migration, of which the experience of the handful of individuals we have just described forms part, has been successful in achieving the goals set for it.

Coincidentally, our attempt to draw a balance-sheet from the results of our own project comes at a time when policy in this field generally is coming under review and the functions performed by the New Towns have been the subject of explicit criticism. To be specific, New Towns policy has been the subject of an extensive examination by the Expenditure Committee of the House of Commons [1]. The Department of the Environment have issued a Consultation Paper on the subject and—in September 1976—an important White Paper summarizing the Government's response to criticisms made by the Expenditure Committee [2].

The aspects of New Towns policy on which attention—and criticism—has focused have tended to be those that have emerged during the course of our own study. The Department of the Environment's Consultation Document, in referring to the admitted problem of housing a more representative cross-section of the urban population, commented that '... to allow the New Towns to beggar the cities they serve by taking only the relatively fortunate members of society and leaving the least fortunate behind would be likely to increase rather than diminish the social problems of those cities' (para. 3.16). The Expenditure Committee, whose members believed that 'much more should be done to relate employment policies to the broader social policies for New Towns' (para. 41), drew the attention of Government Departments to 'the question of the occupational and skill mix in New Towns, to the possibility of encouraging the creation of more unskilled and semi-skilled jobs in New Towns, to training facilities for the unskilled and the unemployed, and to the development of jobs for school-leavers'. They added:

> We have noted the failure of the New and Expanding Towns Scheme (formerly the Industrial Selection Scheme) to operate effectively, and would wish departments to operate a more selective and discriminatory approach to employment policies for New Towns (para. 42).

After drawing attention to the problem of making information available about opportunities to move, the Committee commented that 'the job and housing market are powerful filters through which it is hard for certain groups to pass and concern about (social) balance must therefore be matched by policies that relate not only to job opportunities but also to housing provision' (para. 43). Finally, on the question of the conflict between the goals of housing and employment policies the Committee commented that:

> If housing for employers' needs remains a priority we can see little prospect of a change in New Town allocation patterns. The housing/employment context offers an unfortunate example of the inability of government departments to co-operate to make an impact on what is widely accepted as a major social problem—the tendency for the semi-skilled and the unskilled to be forced to remain in the Inner City. We regret that there appears to be no movement towards (or even interest in) a more selective employment policy to link New Town growth with the problems of the older cities (para. 44).

The main policy issues with which our study has been concerned are therefore for the first time squarely on the policy agenda. However, over and above this new concern with New Towns policy and its objectives, the whole range of planning policies of which the New and Expanding Towns programme forms only part has also been undergoing substantial modification. As we suggested in an earlier chapter, the objectives of the New Towns and the ways in which they have so far been met have been fundamentally affected by the policy context in which they have been set. Indeed, it is arguable that much of the criticism that New Towns are now encountering stems not so much from their performance within that context as from the incompatibility between the broad objectives, as they have been formulated, and the needs of the Inner City and its inhabitants. Before attempting to sum up the significance of our research findings for New Towns policy (as we will try to do in our final chapter) we should therefore begin by briefly considering the changes in the general political and economic climate which have taken place in the recent past, and which have helped to redefine these policy goals.

In Chapter 2, we referred briefly to the origins of the first London New Towns, and their conception and early development as part of a policy of planned dispersal from what was then seen as the over-congested conurbation. Their initial period of active life was marked by a good deal of controversy; and although most of them then began to make their way fairly rapidly, no coherent framework of regional policy existed to set these activities in a policy context. Lloyd Rodwin, reviewing the stage that these 'Mark I' New Towns had reached by the mid-fifties, based his main criticism of their achievement by that date on the absence of such a framework. He commented:

> The original objective of the New Towns Act was to help decentralise London. Other New Towns were authorised later, in response to special problems and pressures. And so the list of designated towns steadily increased. Unfortunately, there were no comprehensive long-term *national* physical development plans. Nor were any undertaken [3].

However, in the early sixties this situation abruptly changed. There were a number of reasons for this about-face; concern at Britain's poor economic performance, after the brief euphoria of the late fifties; and, perhaps more significant, a reversal of previous expectations about population size and distribution, brought about by the unexpected upturn in the birthrate that had begun to appear in the middle fifties and was reinforced by the migration from the Commonwealth which reached a significant level at about the same time. As a response to these new developments, the groundwork for a coherent regional policy was laid down, based initially on a system of controls and incentives elaborated from the concepts first defined in the Barlow Commission Report [4]. This increasingly elaborate apparatus was designed to steer economic growth away from the 'overprivileged' areas—predominantly, again, London and the South-East—towards the 'distressed' areas—initially, the North-East and Scotland. In the course of the sixties and early seventies, however, both the range of incentives and the geographical area of their application steadily widened. Surveying the near-complete structure ten years after construction began, the geographer Michael Chisholm commented on the 'appalling fact' that north of Nottingham and west of the England-Wales boundary 'virtually everywhere is eligible for some form of assistance' [5]. But in the South-East, which has remained throughout outside the circle of beneficiaries, new and more elaborate means of channelling growth of population and employment in the region away from London were set out in a series of regional plans.

This sequence of reports, with their confusingly similar titles, reflects the often confusing evolutions through which regional policy has passed under the impact of changing events. Summarizing very briefly [6], the series begins with the *South-East Study* [7]. This report was based on the fundamental premise that the region would have to accommodate a further $3\frac{1}{2}$ million people in the period from 1961 to 1981, bringing its population from 17.75m. to 21.25m. over the course of that period. Of this increased population, 1.5m. could (it was estimated) be catered for within the scope of existing or planned developments—a quarter of a million of them through the expansion of existing New Towns or Expanding Towns. This left a further 1.5m. to be accounted for; and, in order to cope with this situation without exacerbating the problems of congestion within London or increasing the number of commuters, the authors of the study proposed a further series of New Towns, at a greater distance from London: Milton Keynes, Northampton, Peterborough, and Southampton-Portsmouth. These New Towns were distinguished from their predecessors not only by the distance at which they were to be sited from London, but also by their size (a target population of a quarter of a million, as opposed to 60 000 in the Reith Committee's original conception) and, except in the case of Milton Keynes, by being attached to existing major towns. Commenting on the Plan, and the equivalent documents produced for the West Midlands and the North West, Peter Hall writes:

> These reports of 1963–5 mark an important stage in the evolution of British post-war planning. They recognise officially that the fact of continued population growth demanded positive regional strategies, covering areas that embraced the conurbations and a wide area around them; the reports themselves make it clear that this area extends much further than the conventional 'sphere of influence' defined by geographers in terms of commuting or shopping patterns and may even in some cases approximate to the area of the wider region used for the purposes of economic development planning. These strategies, involving new and expanded towns, were required even for those conurbations in the developments areas ... (but) save for an emphasis on the housing problem, there is little attention to social policy planning; these are still physical plans in a traditional British mould [8].

The *South-East Study* was accepted, in principle, by the incoming Labour Government, which also established a series of regional economic planning councils under the general supervision of the new Department of Economic Affairs. Each of the regions was given responsibility for preparing a regional study and plan; the South-East Planning Council's Report, *A Strategy for the South-East* [9], published in 1967, contained a number of important modifications of the blueprint provided by the *South-East Study*. The 1964 Plan's short-time horizon, and its rather cursory treatment of the question of employment had been the subject of some criticism. For the 1967 Report, proposals were updated and extended to cover the period up to 2001, and their form modified by the proposal to accommodate increased growth along the radial lines of transportation from London, instead of as previously, in the concentric rings inherited from the Abercrombie Plans. These axes were intended to make the best use of existing lines of communication, and to preserve land between the corridors of growth for agricultural and recreational purposes. On employment, *A Strategy for the South-East* endorsed the existing official policy of decentralization, but stressed the need for balance, commenting that new office building—strictly controlled since the Labour Government's emergency 'Brown ban' of November 1964—might sometimes be desirable in London, if the capital was to continue to play its traditional role.

These successive developments in policy represent a considerable contrast with the much narrower objectives of the original New and Expanding Towns policy. Summing up this process, Derek Diamond commented in an essay on the regional context of New Towns that:

> The most obvious explanation of these radical changes lies in the Government revival of interest in regional policy that took place throughout the 1960s. This had several causes; important among them were rapid demographic growth, the slow rate of national economic growth, and widening regional disparities. But also helping to demonstrate the need for a connexion between regional planning and new town development was the changing socio-economic environment of urban living. Increased car ownership, a marked increase in the desired standards of space and amenity, and a rising economic threshold for many public service goods at the local level (i.e. hospitals, schools, shopping centres, cinemas, etc.) all focussed attention on to the question of what is the most appropriate urban form, and hence revived the idea of new towns as experimental urban forms [10].

The next report in the sequence displays some evidence of this change of focus. Entitled *Strategic Plan for the South-East* [11], it was prepared by a team including both central and local government officers, set up jointly by the Government, the Standing Conference on London and South-East Regional Planning and the South-East Planning Council, and published in 1970. This Plan takes some account of the continued rapid decline in London's population (which, the report surmised, might fall as low as 7.3m. by 1981); but it retains the emphasis in the preceding reports on the desirability of creating growth points outside London. The Plan proposes to concentrate these in five major areas—South Hampshire, Milton Keynes-Northampton-Wellingborough, Reading-Basingstoke, South Essex, Crawley-Gatwick, all with a projected future population of half to one and a half million, and supplemented by a number of medium growth areas. On the specific issue of movement of employment from London, the Team comments that:

> an objective of the regional plan should be to stimulate, as appro-

priate, the mobility of employment within the region and to
encourage in particular the further dispersal from London of
employment in both manufacturing and service industries which can
be located satisfactorily elsewhere [12].

However, this line of argument is tempered by the explicit
recognition that one objective of the plan should be to achieve
'the solution of those urgent social and housing problems of
Inner London which have regional implications' [13].

These problems—in all their different aspects—were at the
same time coming under general review as part of the process
of producing the Greater London Development Plan (GLDP).
The Public Inquiry into this Plan, which had been prepared
by the GLC, became the forum in which a whole series of
anxieties could be expressed about the future of London. The
continued rapid decline in London's population was proceeding
at a rate which not only falsified the predictions in successive
regional plans almost as soon as they were made, but gave rise
to additional concern about the composition of the outward flow.
Was London in danger of undergoing the same process of 'social
polarization'—a loss of the 'middle mass', leaving behind a
residue of the prosperous to confront a large number of the very
poor—that some American cities had experienced? The case for
predicting such a fate for London was, at best, debatable; but
what was not in dispute, in the light of new evidence from the
Census, was the extent of the decline in London's manufacturing
employment. In the decade 1961–71 male employment had
fallen by 335 000 (13 per cent of the total). Nor could there
be any doubt about the continuing problems of Inner London,
in terms of housing conditions as well as lost jobs. The *Report
of Studies* for the GDLP (1969) had defined a series of Housing
Stress Areas, covering a substantial proportion of the Inner
Boroughs (including the area examined in the course of the
present study); and evidence was beginning to accumulate that
the steady loss of manufacturing jobs was creating particular
problems for the semi-skilled and unskilled workers in these
areas [14].

As a consequence, the implications of regional policies, as
defined in legislation and amplified in successive plans, began
to be seriously questioned. However, in 1972 when the fieldwork
for the present study was being completed, these questions were

not being explored in any great depth—let alone answered. Indeed, when the Panel of Inquiry into the Greater London Development Plan under Mr Frank Layfield reported to the Secretary of State for the Environment in 1973, they dismissed many of the points raised by the GLC during the course of the Inquiry as either exaggerated or lying outside the capacity of the Council to affect. Nevertheless, concern persisted; the grounds on which it was felt are conveniently summarized in an article published in 1972 by David Eversley, then the GLC's Chief Strategic Planner. Eversley's conclusion was that, in the more limited sense in which it had initially been defined, regional policy had been a success. The Green Belt round London and other major conurbations had held; and the populations of those conurbations had declined substantially. The 'drift to the South-East' had been halted (to the extent that it had ever really existed). But he went on to question whether these developments, in themselves, could be legitimately categorized as successes, arguing that population decline in particular should be reassessed in terms of the disadvantages that it was now likely to produce. He concluded:

> The time has perhaps come when a fundamental reconsideration of the whole problem of old cities and their declining populations should be begun [15].

Events since he wrote that article have further substantially modified the situation, and fully justified the concern he expressed.

Broadly, these further developments have been of three kinds. First, there have been major changes in the economic situation. Second, the demographic picture has gone through yet another series of unexpected shifts. Finally, there have been substantial modifications in the institutional framework within which policies have to be devised. These changes have had consequences of varying kinds at the national, the regional and the London level—which in turn interconnect in ways that are, as we write, the subject of warm disagreement.

On the national level, there is no doubt that the most far-reaching change has been economic. The vast growth in activity in the planning field that took place in the course of the sixties, covering not merely the preparation of regional plans but also the fundamental overhaul of the planning system itself, through the legislation providing for the preparation of structure plans and the reform of local government outside London undertaken in 1972, was all conducted on the premise that continuing economic growth could be taken as given. There was uncertainty, of course, about the level at which growth could be sustained; but none—or next to none—about its persistence. The objectives of planning in every sense of that term— economic, social, land use—were therefore defined in terms of the control and allocation of increased resources [16]. The abrupt change that was brought about by the energy crisis and the decisive shift in the terms of trade against the UK, leading in turn to a sharp deterioration in the balance of payments and accelerating inflation, has totally changed the context in which planning has to take place. In addition to this deterioration in the national economy, certain fundamental structural changes have been taking place within the economy which have important implications for London, and the region as a whole—in particular, the decline in the significance of the manufacturing sector. In addition, alongside these fundamental economic changes population growth has almost completely ceased: the birth-rate has declined substantially, and net immigration has long since come to a halt.

These changes have had important consequences for the South-East region as a whole, not only in the obvious sense that the region and its inhabitants have been directly affected by these developments, but also because they have led to yet another attempt to review the basic assumptions about the role of the region, and London in the region, in the national economy, that have been stated and restated in successive plans. In his announcement of a further review, in November 1974, the Minister for Planning and Local Government observed that:

> he was satisfied that the decision to identify certain areas as suitable for major or medium growth would be fully justified as a means of checking widespread urbanisation throughout the region. While the basic framework of the Plan remained sound, there had been changes in the structure of local government, the economic climate, the cost and availability of fuel and the expected rate of increase in the population of the region. It was time for the Plan to be updated in the light of those and other relevant considerations [17].

At the time at which we write, this exercise has just been completed, and the results published as *Strategy for the South-East: 1976 Review*. The formal responses of central government and the local authorities to the *Review* have not yet been made known, but it is already clear that, despite the Minister's brave words, most of the thinking that lay behind successive Plans has been overtaken by the events that he describes. In the *Report* which was produced by a team similar to the one that undertook the previous exercise, the key issue of population is introduced as follows:

The original SPSE envisaged a population increase of some three million to a total of over twenty million in 1991. The present region, allowing for the transfer of the Bournemouth area to the South West region in 1974 had a population of 16.994 million at the 1971 Census—a growth of 275 000 since 1966—but has since declined by nearly 60 000 to the latest estimated total of 16.936 million in June 1975. Present indications are that, far from increasing over the next 15 years, the region's population is more likely to remain stable and could well decline further ... Recent changes in expectations have, more than any other factor, led both public and private bodies to challenge the growth proposals of the original strategy [18].

In other words, such changes as now seem likely to take place will involve redistribution of population rather than marked growth or decline. 'Current projections', the Team report, 'indicate that London's population could fall by a further 1.4m. by 1991 to 5.7m., whilst that of the rest of the region might increase by 1.6m. to 11.14m' [19].

On the question of resources, the Team predict that 'in the present state of the economy, no growth is likely in the financial resources available to the public sector, even though personal incomes may pick up as the economy improves' [20]. In such a situation, the question naturally arises of priorities in the allocation of such resources as are available. More particularly, debate has centred on the place that London should occupy, within the region, in this new context. The case that London is now suffering from disabilities sufficient to justify its receiving priority within the region—but on a national, as much as on a regional basis—has been energetically advanced, principally by the London local authorities. It has been based

on two premises. First, it is argued that the various processes
of change that have already been touched on are now beginning
to have demonstrably serious consequences for London. The
rapid fall in the conurbation's population (which has already
passed below the point forecast by the 1970 regional report for
1981) has not, in the event, had the kind of beneficial effects
looked for by Howard and his followers from the 'decongestion'
of the metropolis. For one thing, the rapid decline in the total
population has been largely offset by a higher rate of household
formation; young people leave their parents' home earlier, but,
having left, postpone or drastically limit their families. Immigration to London has also added to the number of small,
younger households. At the same time, continually rising
expectations of what housing should offer, in terms of space and
standards, has also added to the level of demand. But, simultaneously, the sharp decline in the size of the privately rented
sector in London has exacerbated the problems facing new
households—and newcomers to London—who are in search of
cheaper accommodation within convenient reach of work. But
perhaps the most important development of all has been the
continued high rate of loss of manufacturing employment. In
the period 1961–74, 34 per cent of manufacturing jobs were lost
in London, compared with a fall of 5 per cent in England and
Wales as a whole. There has, it is true, been a countervailing
gain in employment in the service sector; but this has been lower
in London than in the country as a whole (28 per cent as
compared with 42 per cent), and has not outweighed the decline
in manufacturing industry [21].

This loss of employment opportunities has particularly
affected the unskilled and semi-skilled, as we have already seen;
their increased vulnerability at a time of economic recession is
reflected in residential male unemployment rates of over 10 per
cent in 1975–6 in several Inner London employment exchange
areas. These problems, and the impact that they have had in
the areas affected, sometimes miscalled 'pockets' (in fact, they
contain more people than several of the new Welsh counties)
are of particular relevance for the present study. In a very real
way, these newly increased difficulties sharpen the dilemma of
the inhabitants of areas like North Islington, and in particular
of those without relevant skills who form a substantial proportion
of the population described in Chapter 4. Faced with shrinking

employment opportunities and increasing pressure on housing, as more and more rented housing has fallen either to the municipal bulldozer or the incoming owner-occupier; with no immediate prospect of economic relief—retraining available only to a small minority, and job creation schemes to a handful, at best; the option of moving away from the Inner City's multiple problems would be increasingly attractive, if it became generally available.

However, the second line of the argument deployed on behalf of London has been that the acute problems of the conurbation's inner areas have been exacerbated, not helped, by the regional policies of the past decade, among them the New and Expanding Towns policy, as it has operated over that period. More specifically, it is argued that attempts to constrain economic activity in London by the operation of the IDC policy and steer industry where possible to the assisted areas or to the New and Expanding Towns is no longer appropriate. Moreover, if there are benefits to be obtained from population decline, as such, they have yet to appear—at least, for the remaining inhabitants of the Inner City, who were supposed to be the chief beneficiaries. In David Eversley's picturesque metaphor:

> there is little evidence that this simple-minded bleeding of the cities has done much good, and the cry for yet more leeches to be applied to the urban body should be treated with caution [22].

Against this, it is argued that the process of decline, whatever its consequences, has been largely independent of regional policies: for example, the DSPSE Team quotes from a Department of Industry study that showed that the movement of firms out of London accounted for only 27 per cent of the decline of manufacturing employment between 1966 and 1974, and that only 9 per cent went to assisted areas and 7 per cent to London overspill towns. The largest single component was due to firms closing down completely and not reopening elsewhere. But it could, of course, equally well be argued that given London's present problems, it is unwise to reinforce a process that is inflicting damage.

In their attempts to confront these problems, London local authorities—the GLC and the Boroughs—and those who are thinking along the same lines are acting as advocates; and, to judge by the tone of speeches made by the Secretary of State for the Environment (Peter Shore) in September 1976, they have done so to good effect. But there is one area of policy where the GLC, for one, can take a direct initiative and that is in the sphere of Town Development (policy on town expansion schemes, and the operation of the NETS). During the first half of 1976, the GLC conducted a review of policy in this area, using as a basis for doing so the rethinking of regional priorities then taking place, together with the views of the future shape of New Towns policy that had been expressed by the House of Commons Expenditure Committee, and in the Department of the Environment's Consultation Paper on New Towns [23]. In the Paper produced for this exercise, entitled *Planned Growth Outside London* [24], the GLC reviewed the validity of their own participation in continued efforts to export jobs and population from London, in these changed circumstances. The preliminary conclusion reached was that, subject to negotiation with the receiving authorities, a planned reduction in the rate of migration should take place. At the same time, strong emphasis was laid on the desirability of trying to increase the proportion of the unskilled and those in housing need in the outward flow, along the lines already proposed for the New Towns by the Department of the Environment in its Consultation Paper.

It is in the context of this fundamental questioning of the continued value of the New and Expanding Towns programme that we now turn, finally, to summarizing and drawing out the significance of the findings from our own study.

References

1. Thirteenth Report from the Expenditure Committee, House of Commons, Session 1974/5.

2. Department of Environment, *Consultation Paper on the Future of New Towns* (1975); and *New Towns*: Government Observations on the Thirteenth Report from the Select Committee on Expenditure (Cmnd 6616, HMSO, 1976).

3. RODWIN, LLOYD, *The British New Towns Policy* (Harvard University Press, 1956), p. 63.

4. *Report of the Royal Commission on the Distribution of the Industrial Population* (The Barlow Report) (Cmd 6153, HMSO, 1940).

5. CHISHOLM, MICHAEL, 'Regional Policy for the 1970s', *Geographical Journal*, 140.2, June 1974, p. 218.

6. This discussion draws heavily on PETER HALL, *Urban & Regional Planning* (Penguin Books, 1974). I have also made use of a helpful paper prepared by Ukwu Ejionye, as part of his work for the original project.

7. Ministry of Housing and Local Government, *The South-East Study*, 1961–81 (HMSO, 1964).

8. HALL, op. cit., pp. 170–1.

9. South-East Economic Planning Council, *A Strategy for the South-East* (HMSO, 1967).

10. DIAMOND, DEREK, 'New Towns in the Regional Context' in Hazel Evans (ed.) *New Towns, the British Experience* (Charles Knight, 1972).

11. South-East Joint Planning Team, *Strategic Plan for the South-East* (HMSO, 1970).

12. SPSE, para. 2.55.

13. SPSE, para. 10.2.

14. See especially DANIEL, W. W., *Whatever Happened to the Workers at Woolwich?* (PEP Broadsheet 537, 1972).

15. EVERSLEY, D. E. C., 'Old Cities, Falling Populations and Rising Costs', *GLC Quarterly Bulletin*, March 1972, pp. 5–17.

16. The line of argument here follows that of DAVID EVERSLEY in his *Planning Without Growth* (Fabian Research Series 321, 1975).

17. Department of the Environment, 'Development of the Strategic Plan for the South-East', Interim Report (1976), para. 1.2.

18. Strategy for the South-East: 1976 Review. Report with Recommendations by the South-East Joint Planning Team (HMSO, 1976), para. 3.39.

19. Ibid., para. 3.110.

20. Ibid., para. 3.105.

21. Ibid., para. 4.14.

22. EVERSLEY, *Planning Without Growth*, op. cit., p. 25.

23. Department of the Environment, *New Towns in England and Wales: A Consultation Document* (DOE, December 1974).

24. Greater London Council, *Planned Growth Outside London* (SPB 44), 1976.

Chapter Ten

Conclusions

The Results of the Study

The interviews with those people who have actually succeeded in moving out to a New Town, reported in Chapter 8, represent a conclusion to our study, in more senses than one, since they are at the final point in the process of outward movement that has provided the conceptual framework for the study. In a slightly flippant sense, their individual stories could be taken as providing a happy end to the study; certainly, in describing their successful arrival at the end of the complex passage through the system of selection, it is only right to record the gains that the physical and social environment of the New (and to a lesser extent Expanding) Towns can provide for those moving out of London. However, the fact that they have benefited, as individuals, is not in itself sufficient ground for delivering a favourable verdict on the New or Expanding Towns programme, either in its conception or in the way in which it has functioned in practice. On the contrary, the fact that they are a tiny minority —almost a handful—is in itself a reason for questioning the continued validity of the policy framework.

However, before going on to assess the significance of the findings of this study for the general debate on the future of the New Towns, we shall summarize in the first half of this chapter what we have found out in the course of the study about the movement of the disadvantaged from the Inner City. In the Preface, we gave a list of questions that we hoped at the outset to be able to answer. The simplest way of setting out our findings would be to record the answers that we obtained to each of these questions.

To What Extent did Opportunities to Move prove to Exist?

Only to a limited extent, and then only for selected groups— overwhelmingly, the young and the skilled. In recording this finding, we are doing no more than stating what is already well known, from previous studies (those of Heraud, Roderick and Gee, for example) and indeed from standard statistical sources. To this extent, our study might seem in some danger of repeating the classic pattern of research projects by establishing what is already known, but at wearisome length. However, there was another finding under this general head that we had not expected. This relates to the kind of people within the general category of those qualified to move who were profiting from the opportunity to do so. A very substantial proportion of this group, as the evidence cited in Chapter 6 shows, turned out to be drawn from among the people traditionally regarded (both in British social science and in folklore) as firmly attached to the Inner City locality. These are the 'traditional' local-born manual working class. As we showed in Chapter 6 (Table 6 VII), almost two-thirds of the heads of household in our sample of movers were either born in the Borough of Islington or had lived there for fifteen years or more. Most of them will, of course, have qualified to move by possessing the relevant skills; some will have been further inclined in the direction of moving by the housing circumstances in which they lived in the city; but, even taken together, these two factors do not explain why so many of those who did exercise the option to move are drawn from this group. This finding now appears less surprising, in the light of other, more recent evidence from studies carried out in similar parts of Inner London. For example, Peter Willmott's survey in Central Lambeth, carried out for the Department of the Environment's Inner Area Study, shows a very similar pattern [1]; indeed, it seems possible that the patterns of social change which our study revealed in North Islington may be part of a process affecting Inner London generally.

What were the Obstacles facing the Inhabitants of the Stress Area?

Many obstacles proved to exist; but they varied considerably in character. Arguably, the most significant were those that derive from the basic objectives of planned migration policies and the internal conflicts that have developed within them. We will return to this theme in the second section of this chapter; fundamentally, the problem lies in the form of reconciliation that has been made between the economic objectives of overspill policy—the establishment and maintenance of a sound employment base for the New and Expanding Towns—and the objective of helping Londoners in housing need who are often, as our evidence confirms, semi-skilled and unskilled. The instrument that achieves this reconciliation and with which the individual applicant has to contend, the Industrial Selection Scheme (now NETS), has tended to do so in favour of the first of these. The consequences can be seen, in specific terms, in our evidence; very few indeed of the unskilled in housing need actually moved. There is also recent evidence in confirmation of our findings, from the receiving end, in two studies of a New and an Expanding Town. Audrey Ogilvy's study of Bracknell shows how the proportion of those coming to Bracknell from London declined steadily as the New Town built up—from over 80 per cent in the early fifties to less than half in the sixties. More important for our theme, the migrants that did come from London were drawn from areas and social groups not predominantly in greatest need. She concludes that:

> the New Town had attracted few of those with the lowest incomes among the employed (unskilled workers), few of the household types frequently in economic difficulties (large or one-parent families) and few immigrants to London from overseas—all groups with the worst housing problems in London,

and explains this conclusion by adding that

> the controlling factor, limiting the contribution which the New Town could make to housing problems, was not so much the area from which tenants were drawn but the type of worker able to secure nomination. The channels through which tenants were

recruited favoured selection of people not generally in the most acute housing need [2].

Similarly, Michael Harloe, in his study of the Swindon town expansion scheme, reached the conclusion that although Swindon took just over half its migrants from London, 'many of those in genuine need may have come, not from the hard-pressed areas in the metropolis, but from areas which could possibly have done far more within their own area to solve their inhabitants' housing problems.' Furthermore, the town's policy for recruitment of new industry had a significant effect on the composition of the inflow, since

> the new, expanding firms required a higher proportion of skilled workers than the older, smaller firms. However, these were precisely the sort of people already earning good wages in London, and therefore already well-housed or at least able to look forward to being so reasonably soon. Housing need is highly correlated with unskilled or semi-skilled employment and Swindon had little of this to offer.

As a result,

> Swindon fell somewhere between the New Towns and other Expanding Towns in its value to London as a source of housing for those in greatest need [3].

In addition to this corroboration of the effects of the filtering-out process, as seen from the receiving end, the Greater London Council, in re-analysing the evidence on the proportion of those in housing need who actually succeed in moving as part of their review of policies for planned migration, reached the conclusion that earlier estimates erred on the generous side in assessing the contribution made to the relief of housing need in London. The conclusion reached was that 'only 25 per cent of those moving to New Towns and 32 per cent of those moving to Expanding Towns contributed directly to relieving high priority housing need either by vacating local authority dwellings or because they would have qualified for housing in London had they remained behind' [4].

At a different level, one of the obstacles to movement that seemed at the outset likely to be important in determining people's opportunities to move was the availability of information. We therefore devoted some time to examining people's perceptions of the New Towns and of the opportunities which they had to move there; the results were presented in Chapter 7. The results showed that most inhabitants of the stress area glimpsed their opportunity dimly, if at all. The crucial source of information was through word of mouth, and there was a strong tendency to dismiss the prospect of moving as outside the range of practical possibilities. Moreover, even among those who did know about New Towns, and had gone so far as to explore the ground for themselves, reaction towards making a move were distinctly lukewarm. Clearly, there are missed opportunities here, in terms both of the form and the extent of the diffusion of information about moving [5].

What led to the Decision to Move?

Here, at least, the findings of our study were quite unequivocal. The reasons given for moving were overwhelmingly connected with the improvement of housing circumstances, linked with a better environment (Table 6 XV). In this, the study is in line with earlier investigations—for example that of Frances Gee [6]. Moreover, not merely did migrants give these reasons for moving, they also gave similar reasons for expressing satisfaction in the move, once made (Table 8 III). By contrast, the prospect of finding a better job appeared to count for little—a finding also consistent with earlier evidence, and one of considerable significance, in the light of the importance that employment opportunities play in the planned migration process.

When the reasons given for positively desiring to make a move to a New or Expanding Town were set alongside the respondents' views about their existing place of residence, Islington, some interesting points emerged. As we showed in Chapter 6, there were two significant currents of dissatisfaction with the area. The first could be loosely called 'environmental': complaints about the area being dirty or depressing, becoming noisy or clogged with traffic all attracted significant support among our respondents. The second strand of criticism centred round the theme of change—in part, change in the physical environment as a result of extensive demolition and rebuilding, and in part social change. Some—though not very much—of this concern appears to take the form of open or partly disguised anxiety about the increase in the number of black people. Here again, the findings of our study are very similar to those obtained by Willmott and his colleagues in their study of Central Lambeth.

What were the Intervening Obstacles that caused Failure, in cases where the Decision to move had been taken?

The principal reason to emerge was the sheer complexity of the processes involved in moving. These are described at length in Chapter 3, which draws on a more detailed study undertaken by Charles Thomson [7]; as he shows there, the operation of the mesh within the Industrial Selection Scheme (NETS) helps to perpetuate the bias implicit in the planned migration programme generally, in favour of the skilled working class. As we also show later in the study, there are other means of evading the mesh; movement with migrant firms, for example, or through private networks (the extent of this means of moving was rather greater than we had expected). But these other methods of moving, though not without importance, have not corrected the bias towards the younger skilled families, as examination of the socio-economic composition of the New and Expanding Towns demonstrates.

One possibility among the range of alternative explanations that we set out to examine was that there might be evidence of discrimination against racial minorities. There is no question but that ethnic minorities are under-represented, in proportion to their representation in the population at large, in the New and Expanding Towns. The evidence from the 1971 Census is quite clear on this point:

Table 10 I

Persons born in New Commonwealth, with one or both parents born in New Commonwealth: as proportion of enumerated population

	%
Great Britain	1.7
Greater London	5.7
Eight original New Towns	1.1
Three 'new' New Towns	1.7
Expanding Towns	1.1

Source: 1971 Census

However, the explanation for this situation is less clear. Our own study, which was concerned, in part, explicitly with this question, threw up no evidence of overt discrimination, although it is right to add that we did not examine the attitudes of employers in any detail. In practice, it would be very difficult to operate such a system within the New and Expanding Towns Scheme, since the records kept for the Scheme do not distinguish by race. Nor did we find any evidence to support the allegation that is sometimes made that black workers are deliberately 'shed' by migrant firms moving out of London. But these findings do not necessarily establish that there were no instances where members of minorities were excluded, for superficially legitimate reasons, from the processes of planned migration. Such exclusion, which is termed in current race relations legislation 'indirect' discrimination, could come about as the result of operating the present system without regard to the special difficulties facing minority groups.

One such area of possible 'indirect' exclusion lies in the distribution of information about the opportunity to move; and one of our initial hypotheses was that this factor might be particularly relevant in the case of minorities—either because of language difficulties or the choice of media for providing information about moving. Vigorous attempts have been made to tackle this problem, especially in the case of Milton Keynes but so far without marked success. Our own evidence does go some way to supporting the view that minorities are at a disadvantage in obtaining access to information about New and Expanding Towns but our overall conclusion is that the main difficulty is of a different and rather more fundamental character.

In general, minorities suffer from the same disadvantages as the rest of the Inner City population, in their attempt to move out; and to the extent that a substantial proportion of them are unskilled or semi-skilled, they are blocked in the same way. However, there also appears to be an element of choice. As we saw in Chapter 7, immigrants in the stress area appeared to display a stronger attachment to the area itself than inhabitants of longer standing. This is a finding that seems at first sight rather surprising, given that even in areas of substantial immigrant settlement a great many of the minority groups will not have lived there for more than ten to fifteen years at the most. However, subsequent research (for example, the Report of the

Lambeth Inner Area Study) has confirmed it. Behind this finding lies a most important development—the movement into owner-occupation by minorities that has taken place in the areas of settlement. This process, which had been followed up by a large number of our sample of members of minority groups in the Islington stress area, implies a commitment to the area, in a highly tangible form. Indeed, none of our sample of movers were owner-occupiers—which suggests the strength of the commitment. However, although owner-occupation does offer the best opportunity for newcomers to improve their immediate housing circumstances, it should not be assumed that they thereby obtain access to facilities on a par with those enjoyed by established owner-occupiers in the white population. In fact, as David J. Smith shows [8], West Indian owner-occupiers are significantly worse off, in terms of amenities and overcrowding, than their equivalents in the population at large. Nevertheless, owning a house remains the simplest way of escaping from the far worse conditions in the private rented sector, which we describe in Chapter 5. It is therefore unlikely to be coincidental that the one London New Town, Crawley, that provided a significant opportunity to become an owner-occupier upon moving is also the one with a significant Asian population [9].

One other potentially disadvantaged minority has fared somewhat better than we would have expected, in a system in which suitability for employment has tended to be the major determining factor. The elderly, by virtue of special arrangements made to cater for them, have been adequately represented in the migration stream. In fact, 13 per cent of new tenancies in the established London New Towns between 1966 and 1973 went to elderly tenants [10].

The unbalanced nature of the composition of the migration has been the subject of repeated comment, and of a number of attempts at correction: the attempt to create Special Housing Allocations in the sixties, the failure of which in Bracknell is well described by Audrey Ogilvy; and now the attempts to bypass the New and Expanding Towns Scheme by making direct arrangements between the new New Towns and selected London boroughs. We will consider this issue in greater detail later in this chapter.

What was the Reaction of those who Succeeded in reaching the New or Expanding Towns?

This is the question to which we addressed ourselves in Chapter 8. If the picture that we present there is indeed a representative one (and we must necessarily be cautious about reaching any conclusions on the basis of such a small sample), the answer seems clear-cut. Those who persist through all the administrative complexities reap their reward in the form of the environmental and housing gains that provided the main motive force for migration. There are, in fact, only three qualifications to be made: first, that increased costs—and the exacerbating difficulty of finding employment for wives—have undoubtedly caused problems in some cases; and, second, that certain facilities associated with the City—access to shops and entertainment, in particular—are missed. The third qualification is of a different order; the satisfaction that we report may not extend to some of the town development schemes, where there is evidence to show that for a variety of reasons, satisfaction may not be so great. With these qualifications, it seems fair to say that we found no grounds to support the commonly held belief about the 'New Town blues'; on the contrary, within their own terms, the New Towns, at least, seemed to us to have earned their admiring summer crowds of visiting Japanese planners and Argentinian highway engineers.

However, before accepting this satisfied consumers' verdict on the outcome of the process of planned migration, we should pause to consider more precisely how success is best measured. The satisfaction that our respondents reported is, it is true, generally confirmed by the evidence from other similar enquiries. Moreover, the objective evidence on the collective performance of the New and Expanding Towns, if taken in isolation, is undeniably impressive. Between 1946 and 1975, the New Towns provided 200 000 homes for 700 000 people. One house in thirty-five built between the end of the Second World War and 1975, and one house in twenty built in the public sector, has been built in a New Town. Town development schemes have provided 85 000 local authority houses for quarter of a million people, over the same period—150 000 of them Londoners. Since designation, some sixty million square feet of factory floor space have been built in New Towns, providing employment for quarter of a million people, together with forty million square feet in Expanding Town schemes. Over the same period, seven million square feet of office space have been provided in New Towns. The Department of the Environment estimates that 'by the end of the century at least 2½m. people will have been housed in schemes designed to promote planned migration' [11].

But when these statistics are set in the context of the contribution of the New and Expanding Towns to the solution of the social and economic problems of the conurbations, they take on a different significance. For, as we saw in Chapter 4, the problems of the Inner City—and Inner London in particular—have persisted throughout the period of the New Towns' achievements; indeed, in some respects they are arguably worse. Graham Lomas' account of the concentrations of housing and employment stress in Inner London, and the intensifications in each produced by the interaction between them provides conclusive supporting evidence [12]. As far as London is concerned, a steady drop in the population—even one protracted over almost the entire course of the century—and thirty years of an officially supported planned migration policy have failed to produce the amelioration in the metropolis' situation that Ebenezer Howard saw as the key objective of policy. Seen in this light, the statistics of the New Towns' success story in the employment field are not reassuring; rather, they are salt in London's wounds.

The Significance of the Findings

At this point, it might be helpful to review briefly the accumulated evidence from the study, in the context of the 'managerialist' thesis set out in Chapter 1—and more particularly the four explanatory models that were described there.

Taking the '"pure" managerialist thesis' first, this suggests that the control of resource allocation is entirely in the hands of professional officers or 'urban managers'. It is certainly true that the way in which the New Towns programmes have developed has been affected by professional attitudes towards them. The New Towns grew up alongside the planning profession; and have for a generation been regarded as the epitome of the success that can be achieved by a rational application of the principles taught in planning schools. As a result, it is to be expected that individual planners of the generation now occupying senior positions in local and central government will tend to view New Towns somewhat uncritically. Similarly, now that regional policy and its objectives have come to be regarded as an intrinsic part of the processes of government, New Towns tend to be viewed indulgently by economists and geographers, either within government or influential with it, as instruments for achieving regional economic growth. More generally, as we saw in Chapter 2, the way in which New Towns have developed has been influenced by the sustained evangelism of Ebenezer Howard's followers. The evident success of the pioneer New Towns not only provided the justification for that campaign, but fixed in the minds of the lay public to whom it was directed, an influential image: New Towns as successful experiments in social engineering, produced by the initiative of a few remarkable individuals (Howard, Osborn, Reith) working outside the traditional political framework. These men—and the more orthodox politicians who worked with them, like Lewis Silkin— were gate-builders, rather than gatekeepers; but their example has patently influenced those who play humbler roles in the political process.

It is, however, difficult to say just how far such pressure groups and influential individuals have affected the actual situation of New Towns policy. For one thing, the power of both the planners and the evangelists is circumscribed in practice by other less Utopian considerations. Nevertheless, all these groups participate vigorously in discussion about the future direction of policy—as in the case of the current debate between the Greater London Council and the London Boroughs Association on the one hand, and the New Town Association, the Development Corporations and the Town and Country Planning Association on the other.

Turning to the implementation of policy decisions and allocation of resources, it could certainly be argued that individual managers have power to affect the chances of individuals to obtain a home in a New Town—that they are, precisely in Pahl's terms, the 'urban gatekeepers'. This does not, however, seem to be a satisfactory explanation of the situation we have studied. It is true that a large proportion of those who might want to move to a New or Expanding Town (and might profit from doing so) are indeed turned back at the gate—if we use that term to cover the procedure through which moves take place, principally the New and Expanding Towns Scheme (NETS). However, their rejection is not usually the result of decisions taken by individual allocators of resources. Desk clerks and housing visitors (even housing managers) may take steps that have important consequences for individual applicants; but the fundamental causes of rejections stem from the objectives which the system of allocation is set up to meet. The fact that its very complexity is sometimes a reason why individual applications fail to succeed is a reflection of the complex—and potentially conflicting nature of these objectives.

Thus, in our view, the answer to the question 'who allocates?' is not unequivocally suggested by the 'pure' managerialist model. Other features come closer to those suggested by both the 'statist' and the 'control-by-capitalists' model. Taking the 'statist' model first, there is no doubt that national government is directly involved in New Towns policy at many levels. Because New Towns (unlike Expanding Towns) stand largely outside the structure of local government, the impetus for new designations comes principally from the centre. Plans for New Towns are devised, shelved or revived by national government, depending, to a large extent, on factors like the level and distribution of public expenditure and central forecasts of future population trends. At the operational level, as we saw in Chapter 3, the Department of Industry can impose limits on the type and size of firms that can move and the areas in which they can relocate. In this way, central government intervenes to strike a policy balance between the industrial and employment needs of different areas. Moreover, in an important reformulation of New Towns policy, the Secretary of State for the Environment, Peter Shore, outlined in September 1976 the government's intention to tilt the balance of industrial location policy in favour of the exporting authorities who are losing population and jobs; geographically, in favour of the Inner City and its inhabitants. The implication of his speech is that just as restrictions on the movement of firms to London's Docklands have been very recently relaxed to bring them into line with New Towns in the South East, so 'the incentives to industrial location (can) be better tuned to assist in inner areas, without disturbing regional policy.' Thus, we can expect that very shortly central government will introduce measures designed to give declining inner cities as legitimate a claim to whatever firms are considering relocation as the Development Areas and New and Expanding Towns already have.

But as the Secretary of State himself admitted:

> We have only limited power directly to create the industries, large or small, privately or publicly owned, on which the wealth of these areas will be based. All industries and firms are bound to take their location decisions according to which is likely to produce the best return. Our effort must primarily be directed not so much to making those decisions but to influencing them, either in favour or against the inner areas [13].

This statement underlines an important point: that the effectiveness of government policies is constrained by the desires of entrepreneurs and industrial managers to obtain maximum 'return' or profit. The 'control-by-capitalists' model, in this sense, holds true in that public authorities, be they local or national, have to allow industry, acting in what is conceived to be its own best interests, to come to them. Government can both apply planning restrictions and supply incentives: but, in a mixed economy with a substantial private sector it is broad economic measures, rather than narrower policies linked to specific locations, that will be the more influential—subject to the limitations on the effectiveness of all central government policy in this field during the post-war period. In this perspective, it is the state of the economy and the operation of decision-making within the framework of the functioning of the economy that largely determine who moves, and where, and who is employed and where. But the 'control-by-capitalists' model seems to be used in two further senses: first, that, as Castells suggests, government acts on behalf of capitalist enterprise and this is an exhaustive explanation of government policies; secondly, that the operation of New Towns policies is moulded entirely by the desires of capitalist enterprise. As far as the first proposition is concerned, this study can provide no supporting evidence. As we have already indicated, our study was not intended to cover the subject from this perspective: but it does seem clear from the evidence that we have gathered that there is ample scope for a study that would adopt it.

As for the second proposition—that it is the operation of New

Towns policy which succours and is controlled by capitalists: it is of some relevance that it is very difficult for a tenant to move into a Development Corporation house without first securing a job in a New Town. In this sense, priority is given to suitable labour rather than suitable tenants and it is clearly industry that calls the tune. Nevertheless, some considerable efforts are made to give priority to those in housing 'need' or to those, such as current council tenants, who might make way for those with housing problems. Thus, the situation is not a starkly simple one, for it is mediated by urban managers who do have explicitly different priorities from employers. The efficiency, however, with which urban managers can combine the labour needs of firms with the housing needs of families is, as we have seen throughout this study, not very great.

Finally, we come to the 'pluralist' model, which posits a 'permanent tension' between 'national bureaucracies', 'private capital', and 'the political party representing the dominant class'. On the whole, as we suggested might be the case in Chapter 1, we do not consider our study confirms this model. For these three institutions are not locked in perpetual battle over the direction and operation of New Towns policy, nor do they necessarily and inevitably serve discrete interests. The rapid development of New Towns and, subsequently, Expanding Towns under post-war Labour governments has clearly had the support of both 'national bureaucracies' and 'private capital'; each group may have supported the policy for rather different reasons, but nevertheless they appeared to act in concert most of the time. Indeed, the current controversy about overspill appears to be argued out *between* politicians and *between* national bureaucracies; for, irrespective of party, politicians tend to defend the interests of their constituencies be they Inner City areas in the South-East region or the development areas of the North-East. The point is that, in practice, the objectives of New Towns policy appear to conflict: 'self-containment' is to some extent incompatible with provision for 'housing need', and it is far from certain whether the development of successful regional economic multipliers will provide housing, a good working environment and employment for the poor, and often unskilled, Inner City residents. Given this situation, it is inevitable that different bureaucratic interest groups will spring up to defend particular elements in New Towns policy.

Thus, while the 'urban managerialist thesis' could, in principle, shed some light on the factors behind the direction and intentions of New Towns policy, it does not yet provide a consistent basis on which to analyse this policy. It does, however, lead us to ask the key question 'who gains?' And if our evidence demonstrates one thing for certain it is that the deprived Inner City population does not figure prominently among the beneficiaries of existing policy—a fact now recognized, and endorsed by recent shifts in the direction of policy. The crucial test—which will have the incidental consequence of helping to illuminate the debate about the causes of the present distribution of benefits—is how far these changes will prove to be effective in practice.

Where Next?

As we saw in the previous chapter, fundamental criticisms of the policies designed to achieve planned overspill have been steadily accumulating, as part of the general re-appraisal of the objectives of physical and social planning that has taken place in the middle seventies. This criticism can be seen in its harshest form in Michael Harloe's summary of evidence from his Swindon study, which we have already cited. He concludes that New Towns 'can only make a marginal contribution to the relief of housing need, and will probably never offer a solution to the hard core of need in the conurbations.' Although his verdict on the performance of Expanding Towns is slightly more favourable, he adds that 'little of value remains in the claim which, more than any other, inspired the adoption of the overspill programme by the national government after the last war, namely that New and Expanding Towns could play a strategic role in the relief of industrial congestion, poor evironment and housing need in the major British cities' [14].

These criticisms have been echoed, if not always in so severe a form, by other critics. Milton Keynes, the flagship of the London-related new New Towns, has been the target of repeated criticism in the press, principally on the theme of wrong priorities in the allocation of scarce resources [15]. Nor have these criticisms been confined to the London New Towns. Like the GLC, the upper-tier authorities in the Midlands and Lancashire have become increasingly concerned about the consequences of the continued build-up of New Towns in their vicinity, and the relationship between this process and the problems of the deprived inner areas. As early as 1971, Birmingham City Council took a decision to reverse their original policy of encouraging migration of people and industry to New Towns and partici- pating in Town Development schemes, in view of continued high levels of unemployment in inner areas. Largely as a result of this kind of questioning of the implications of planned migra- tion policies, the future of the New Town in Central Lancashire is now in doubt. But most drastic of all has been the criticism levelled at the Scottish New Towns. The *Development Strategy* produced by Strathclyde Regional Council concluded that the growth of the New Towns in the region had been 'at the expense ... of the older areas which are in need of renewal and the evidence of socio-economic structure shows that the New Towns have not really catered for the disadvantaged groups from those urban areas. This has accentuated a high concentra- tion of deprivation in these areas ... (para. 10.40)' [16]. In 1976, the Secretary of State for Scotland conceded the logic of the argument by deciding not to proceed with the New Town at Stonehouse, and to devote the resources released in this way to an extensive scheme for the regeneration of Inner Glasgow. The significance of Mr Millan's decision was subsequently con- firmed both by the Government's White Paper on New Towns [17], which made it clear that there would be no further designations for at least five years, and by Peter Shore's speech of September 1976, in the course of which he announced an inquiry into the consequences of planned and unplanned migra- tion from inner cities.

Some evidence that a real modification will occur has already emerged. The GLC's policy review produced a wide range of responses, adopting one or other (or in some cases several) of the lines of response described above. As a result of further consultations, the Council did modify the emphasis in their original recommendations, on the issue of further Government investment in New Towns in particular; but their broad con- clusion stood—that the level of the Council's commitment to planned migration would have to be reduced, by 'natural wastage', as the town development agreements which the Council had made with other authorities were allowed to expire without being renewed.

At the same time, the Department of the Environment have also reviewed their position. First, the Minister of Local Government and Planning has introduced amending legislation that would implement the proposal in the Department's Consultation Paper [18] and transfer the ownership of housing in 'mature' New Towns from the Development Corporation to the relevant local authority. More significant for our present theme, the Department also issued new guidance in April 1976 to the 'active' New Towns on the allocation of tenancies by Development Corporations. Introducing their review (NT Circular 445), the Department referred both to the problem of imbalance in the social structure of New Towns, and to the need to give proper weight to the housing in New Towns of Londoners in housing need. It is suggested that the principle that housing should only be offered to those who will work within the designated area of the New Town can now be relaxed, and that this may be of assistance in absorbing a wider range of social categories. A series of priority categories for housing is then proposed: the first two in the top priority group are Londoners in housing need—the second of these two being cases where there is no requirement for employment. However, the balance between these and other categories, including workers with migrant firms, is left to local discretion. In putting these guidelines forward, the Department also indicate their intention to monitor the effects of this change of policy in practice.

Meanwhile, several of the new New Towns have been promoting direct links with individual London boroughs, thereby circumventing the NETS procedure which, like the House of Commons Expenditure Committee, some Development Corporations appear to have come to see as a cumbersome and inefficient means of achieving movement from London. Considerable stress has been placed by Inner London boroughs, in concluding these agreements, on the desirability of securing a larger proportion of their local population in need in the outflow; and this emphasis has been generally accepted by the Corporations.

Finally, the White Paper issued by the Department of the Environment in September 1976 ties all these initiatives together, in what amounts to a declaration of intent. While there are to be no further designations of New Towns in the immediate future, existing towns will 'give a new priority to housing the old and disadvantaged from the Inner City'. Measures will be taken to achieve closer collaboration between the Government Departments concerned, and to secure consistency between policy objectives in different relevant policy areas. Gaps in the availability of research findings will be plugged, and the whole programme subject to annual review by the Department of the Environment.

What all this implies, in practical terms, remains to be seen. But it is open to doubt whether changes of this kind can be in any sense fundamental in their effects. As long as the emphasis on the New and Expanding Towns programme is ultimately determined by the objective of securing the economic viability and social equilibrium of the receiving areas, so long will there be limits placed on the contribution that the New and Expanding Towns can make to the solution of the economic and social problems of the conurbations.

References

1. SHANKLAND COX, with Institute for Community Studies, *London's Inner Area: Problems and Possibilities* (Department of the Environment, 1976).

2. OGILVY, A. A., *Bracknell and its Migrants: twenty-one years of a New Town's growth* (HMSO, 1975), pp. 59 and 62.

3. HARLOE, MICHAEL, *Swindon: A Town in Transition* (Heinemann, 1975), p. 270.

4. Greater London Council, *Planned Growth Outside London* (Report SPB 44, 1976), para. 39.

5. For a full account of this problem, see GOLD, J. R., *Communicating Images of the Environment* (CURS Occasional Paper No. 29, 1974).

6. GEE, FRANCES, *Homes and Jobs for Londoners in New and Expanding Towns* (HMSO, 1972).

7. THOMSON, CHARLES, *The Industrial Selection Scheme*, op. cit.

8. SMITH, DAVID J., *The Facts of Racial Disadvantage* (PEP Broadsheet 560, 1976).

9. This was the New Town studied by Audrey Maxwell, as part of our original project.

10. Cited by E. Armstrong, in the House of Commons debate on the New Towns (Amendment Bill), 23 March 1976, at Col. 333.

11. Department of the Environment, Occasional Paper No. 4, *Planned Migration to New and Expanded Towns* (1975), p. 4.

12. LOMAS, G. et al., *The Inner City* (London Council of Social Service, 1975).

13. *Inner Urban Problems:* Speech by Secretary of State for Environment in Manchester, 17 September 1976.

14. HARLOE, op. cit., pp. 283–4.

15. BROOKER, C., 'Shoring Up Planning Disaster', *Spectator*, 2 October, 1976.

16. Strathclyde Regional Council, *Development Strategy* (April 1976).

17. Department of the Environment, *New Towns*, Government observations on the Thirteenth Report from the Select Committee on Expenditure. House of Commons Paper 616, Session 1974–5 (Cmnd 6616, HMSO, 1976).

18. Department of the Environment, *New Towns in England and Wales*, op. cit.

Appendices

A Note on the Two Estates in Milton Keynes

The workers from the firm in question had been rehoused on two estates that will eventually be incorporated into the new city of Milton Keynes. The larger estate—on which twenty-seven ex-Londoners who worked for the firm lived—had been built by Bletchley UDC and the GLC as part of the town expansion scheme. The smaller estate—on which eleven former Londoners lived—had been originally built by Wolverton UDC, but a number of the houses had been taken over by the Milton Keynes Development Corporation. This afforded a useful comparison between an estate built near an already sizeable shopping and communications centre and a much smaller estate built near a small market town.

Moreover, interesting comparisons could be made between the two estates since one houses approximately 4000 people and the other about 400: the question of size could therefore be tackled both from the point of view of the towns to which these estates were attached and the estates themselves.

The larger estate—on which most of the workers from this particular firm were housed—was very large indeed. A population of 4000 was served by two primary schools, a secondary school, and a small number of shops, many of which were not yet complete. The main shopping centre was in Bletchley $1\frac{1}{4}$ miles away. The estate was still being built when the researcher visited it, but since the first house had been built three years before, it had had a chance to develop its own identity. A community newspaper and community forum, started by the three local community workers, helped to cement community feeling and newcomers were welcomed by an information sheet which listed nineteen organizations which had organizers actually living on the estate. These organizations covered, amongst other things, the Bletchley Skating Club, two Brownie packs, the community newspaper, the angling club and the estate senior citizens' club. The local social committee organized dances once a month during the winter.

This larger estate looked from the outside, and at first glance, to consist of row upon row of box-like terraces. Respondents who had rejected the idea of living on this estate referred to them as 'barracks' and Development Corporation architects tended to pour scorn on their design. Seen from the railway line—which runs very close to it—it seems a poor introduction to the Utopian ideals behind much of the new city's design—it looks forbidding and uniform. However, the houses and bungalows—which are of four types—are built around small cul-de-sacs, all of which end in very generous and well-planted open space. In fact, once in the estate and walking around it, the general impression—at least in the summer—is of light, openness, and space well used for sitting in, playing cricket, football, or car maintenance. Nor is the uniformity of the buildings overwhelming, since the different dwelling types are well distributed, and there is a good network of footpaths which link the different 'places', 'closes', 'groves' and 'avenues' with each other. A major road runs alongside the estate and forms one of the boundaries of the designated area. On the other side of the road is the kind of English countryside beloved of the British Tourist Authority with many footpaths and a well-fished canal. This was the area which many of the respondents could see from their bedroom windows and spoke of with pride and affection and hopes that it would not be built upon.

The smaller estate was ten miles north and because of its size and design looked much more conventionally 'homely'. The houses were mainly in terraces, fairly unimaginatively arranged along side roads. The estate itself was on the edge of Stony Stratford and, in fact, about half of it was occupied by UDC tenants and our respondents were in the more recently built dwellings put up by the UDC and purchased from them by the Development Corporation. When I accompanied the workers on one of the trips their firm organized to the town before the move, this little estate seemed to me, and I felt, to many of the other workers to be the more attractive. Its smaller size implied less anonymity, the houses looked more attractive from the outside, and its location was much nearer the new warehouse than the other estate. Even though the rents were just over £1.00 higher, the savings on transport to and from work would almost absorb this extra expense. Thus for those who managed to get houses on this little estate the future looked rosy, since it seemed they would be entering a neighbourly world on the edge of what was once, and no doubt will be again once the Development Corporation has improved it, a quite charming mainly nineteenth-century country town. But when I went round it the second time, its appeal had worn a little thin since, in contrast to the larger estate, it seemed closed in—even claustrophobic. There was hardly any public open space within the estate, and what there was was known as the 'wreck' and was a largely concreted-over mound for children. The only green open space was either on the other side of an extremely busy main road or at the back of the estate where the building of new roads and a Development Corporation estate was rapidly approaching the back gardens of some of the houses in which the respondents lived. This lack of public open space was criticized by the respondents but to me it also had the effect of preventing the feeling of 'cosiness' and 'community' which I had felt as I walked along the footpaths of the larger estate. This may have been a false impression but since on the smaller estate there was nowhere for the children to kick a ball or the mothers to watch them except in the road, the immediate opportunities for the formation of small informal groups which felt comfortable and not harassed by traffic did not exist. On the larger estate they did, and before tea-time I could see groups of small children and fathers kicking balls and mucking about with motor cars.

In fact, to my initial surprise, the two estates turned out to contrast with each other in unexpected ways. And this was not just my impression but confirmed, on the whole, by the comments of most of the respondents. Those on the smaller estate complained frequently and vehemently about the lack of play-space for the children and the awkwardness of access to the nearest open space. They also complained about the shops—their prices and lack of choice, variety and competition.

In summary, people felt that the town had not been prepared for them. A respondent complained that pavements were not wide enough to cater for prams side by side, and others complained that there were not enough pillar boxes and they were cut off from the cheap return services to London from Bletchley.

In fact, it seemed to me that the two estates nicely illustrated the importance of one of the social goals of the new city: namely, the goal of choice and variety. The larger estate provided many of the amenities needed by all the New and Expanding Town dwellers and it could do this partly because of its convenient location near a sizeable well-equipped town, partly because it was built for an influx of young strangers and hence had been designed with children in mind, but also—and probably more importantly—because its size was big enough to generate its own internal services. The shops, the two integral schools, the two planned pubs and health centres provided for easy access, choice on the doorstep and further choice was available in the more distant but still accessible local high street. There was choice in other ways as well. While it is true to say that at the time I spoke to these families, many of them were very close indeed to friends drawn from within the firm with which they had all moved, the larger estate provided for the establishment of a wider network of friends and also provided the social organizations where people could meet. On the smaller estate, that choice will never be available and the local organizations were entirely based on the original town which seemed to resent the influx of newcomers. This local tension had apparently been made clear in the parent/teachers association of the local primary school. It is, of course, possible that this difficulty will be resolved when the nearby Development Corporation estate is completed, but this will rather depend on whether the community workers on that estate work for the integration of the two. One respondent on the small estate complained that they would not be able to send their children to the schools on the adjoining estate, which bodes badly for integration and, as a result, she and her husband were anxious to exchange their present house for one on this new estate. Thus, on the smaller estate there was much more evidence of the 'New Town blues' with the traditional complaints of lack of services and isolation.

The Methodology of the Two Social Surveys

This Appendix draws heavily on the two methodological reports published by Social and Community Planning Research, who carried out the surveys and tabulations. The two reports are: Ellen Johnson, *Inner London Study: Methodological Report* (SCPR, 1972); and Jean Morton-Williams, *Study of Migrants from Islington: Methodological Report* (SCPR, 1972).

I The Stress Area Survey

This survey was carried out in January and February 1972 after a small pilot survey in November 1971. The survey consisted of structured interviews with 512 heads of household living in the Tollington district (Parkway and Station wards) of the London Borough of Islington.

Sampling

SCPR designed the sampling methodology in conjunction with Garry McDonald. The universe, which comprised four polling districts in the Tollington area of Islington, was selected purposely to cover a particular social structure of the Borough. In order to obtain a general population sample, we obtained the four Electoral Registers covering the chosen district.

A known fault of the Electoral Register is that it fails to cover certain groups of the population adequately, notably Commonwealth citizens, young voters and people in new buildings; all groups of considerable importance to the study. It was therefore necessary to take steps to make good these deficiencies if serious bias was to be avoided. Prior to sampling, SCPR sent three enumerators into the field to look for addresses which were omitted from the register. Enumerators were given written instructions and forms on which they were to record missing addresses. Each form contained a photocopied portion of the Electoral Register, which the enumerators were to check. Their task was not to contact any residents personally, but to assess the situation by observation. The most common omissions which could be detected were flats in either converted or purpose-built blocks, where the flat number was clearly marked, and new buildings. Commercial property was excluded unless residential accommodation was obviously integrated.

Even though this check on the Registers could not be designed to be comprehensive, the results proved that there were indeed significant omissions. The proportion of addresses which were excluded from the Register ranged from 8 per cent to 17 per cent in the four polling districts. The particularly high figure of 17 per cent was in a district with an extensive programme of public building which was not completed at the time of the publication of the Register. In addition, several buildings were found to have been demolished in one particular polling district. The high proportions of under-representation can be explained to some extent by the redevelopment plans in the area but, nevertheless, it was still surprising to find more than 4–5 per cent omissions. The figures are detailed below:

Omitted Addresses

	Number	%	Number demolished
Parkway K	82	8	1
Parkway L	110	8	15
Highbury A	72	10	2
Highbury B	109	17 (incl. new building)	—

The data collected by the enumeration procedure were used to correct the Registers. A sample of addresses was then drawn from the Registers. In order to give each address an equal chance of inclusion, the following procedure was used:

(i) The four Registers were placed together as if they comprised one area.

(ii) Then the total number of electors were divided by the number of desired interviews (i.e. 500), adding sufficient extra interviews to allow for non-response. The result of this division became the sampling interval.

(iii) A random number was selected which was less than the sampling interval, to locate the starting point to begin drawing the sample.

(iv) Next, the electors were counted off at equal intervals throughout the four wards. The address at which the elector resided was included in the sample only if the elector was the first person listed at that address. This ensured that addresses with several electors had no greater chance of inclusion than those with only one elector.

(v) This method resulted in a sample of 704 addresses which represented approximately 1 in 7 of all addresses in the area.

The sampling of addresses was then converted, by the interviewer at the doorstep, into a sample of households. This procedure can only be undertaken on the spot as the Register does not indicate the number of households at an address. The interviewers were provided with special forms on which they had to list the surname of the head of household for each household resident at the address. However, it is customary to limit the number of interviews to no more than three at an address for practical interviewing reasons. These three could be chosen by the interviewers as the bias created by their choice would be small. Once the three were selected, the interviewer was instructed to pursue these three only and to make no substitutions.

Using this method of converting a fixed number of addresses into a variable number of households meant that the number of households to be interviewed was increased beyond that required. In order to reduce the number of households without introducing bias, the interviewer was instructed to delete the next uncontacted address from her issued quota for each additional household found at an address; if two households were found at address A, one address was struck off the issued sample; if three households were found, the next two addresses were struck off. If there were no uncontacted addresses, then the additional interviews created by multi-occupancy were continued. This procedure resulted in a final sample of heads of household equal to the number of issued addresses. In practice, the limit of three households at an address did not significantly bias the sample as only 2 per cent of addresses contained four or more households.

Response rates

Initially 704 addresses were issued in order to achieve approximately 500 interviews with heads of household. In fact, the achieved number of completed interviews was 512, which was derived as follows:

Issued Addresses	704	100%		
plus Multi-household Addresses	230	33%		
minus Addresses Deleted to Compensate for Multi-household Addresses	202	29%		
Deadwood*	32	4%		
Qualifying Households	700	99%	=	100%
minus Refusals	70			10%
No contact after 4 calls	66			9%
Sick	15			2%
Language Difficulties	14			2%
Away for Survey Duration	12			2%
Other reasons	8			1%
Total Non-Response:	185			26%
Interviews	515			74%
minus Unusable questionnaires	3			ø
Final Sample	512			73%

(ø = less than 0.5%)

As expected, there was a high proportion of multi-household addresses in this area: 55% of productive interviews were at multi-household addresses.

* Deadwood consists of addresses which turned out to be empty, demolished or non-residential. The bulk of these were empty premises, a fault undetectable in the earlier enumeration procedure.

Data preparation

Questionnaires were edited and coded by members of SCPR's Survey Unit. In order to code the many open-ended questions, code lists were drawn up based on content analysis of the first fifty questionnaires. The derivation of the final code-lists was undertaken by SCPR in co-operation with the researcher.

When coding was complete, the data were transferred to eighty-column punch cards using two cards per respondent. The cards were then submitted to a complete computer edit procedure designed to check on the accuracy of the coding, consistency of responses and correct filtering procedures.

Analysis specifications were decided by the researcher with the advice of SCPR. Analysis was preceded by a hole count on all columns. The data were analysed by five main standard variables, Family Type, Income, Socio-Economic Groups, Birthplace of Head of Household, and Length of Residence in Islington.

II The Migrants' Survey

This survey was of 201 heads of household who had moved from the London Borough of Islington to a New or Expanding Town in the previous five years. The fieldwork took place in July and August, 1972.

Sampling

Lists of people who had moved from Islington to New or Expanding Towns since 1967 were supplied by the GLC. Because of budgeting considerations and the small sample size, it was not possible to sample at random from these lists as this would have resulted in a very large number of sampling points, some with a very few names within them, entailing an uneconomic amount of travelling on the part of the interviewers. It was decided to confine the interviewing to ten New or Expanding Towns to be selected from among those with fifty or more listed people in them. In the event, there were only nine towns containing fifty or more people on the lists supplied by the

GLC: a tenth town was added by taking the one with the next highest number of names; this was Haverhill with thirty-nine names.

Except for Haverhill where all the names supplied were used, fifty names were selected from those supplied for each town using a random procedure.

The response rate could not be accurately predicted since a fairly high but unknown proportion were expected to have moved again since they first went to the New or Expanding Town. Since it was important to confine the sample size to about 200 interviews to keep within the costs, a procedure was used by which two fifths of the sample in each town were marked as reserves; this yielded a preliminary sample of just under 300 names which were tackled first by the interviewers in order to give an accurate picture of co-operation and the proportion who had moved. When all the names on the preliminary list had been accounted for, the interviewers moved on to their reserve list and continued until they had achieved about twenty interviews in the town or had exhausted their reserve list. Inevitably the recalling on the reserve sample was less stringent than for the primary sample.

Response rates

Response rates, for the primary and reserve samples are given separately.

	Primary Sample		Reserve Sample	
	No.	%	*No.*	%
Number of names issued	285	—	205	—
Called on	285	100	105	51
Interviews achieved	158	55	46	44
Not interviewed	127	45	59	56
Reasons for non-response				
Moved	69	25	32	30
Premises empty/person unknown	14	5	4	4
No contact after 3 or more calls				
(one or more calls for reserve sample)	26	9	16	15
Refused/ill	7	2	2	2
Away for fieldwork period	7	2	4	4
Miscellaneous	2	1	1	1
Ineligible (not from Islington)	2	1	—	—
	127	45	59	56

As can be seen from the analysis of the primary sample response rate, about a quarter of those listed had moved. Interviewers were asked where possible to find out from the present residents where the named person had moved to. Unfortunately, in a large proportion of the cases they were not able to do so; the information obtained for all those who were found to have moved in both the primary and reserve samples is given below:

	No.	%
Total who had moved	101	100
Moved elsewhere in the same town	16	16
Moved back to London	14	14
Moved elsewhere	10	10
Not known where moved to	61	60

The towns in which the interviewing took place and the numbers of interviews achieved in each were as follows:

Towns	No. of interviews
Ashford	21
Basildon	22
Basingstoke	25
Bletchley	21
Harlow	9
Haverhill	18
Letchworth	21
Stevenage	24
Wellingborough	21
Witham	19
	201

The reason for the low response rate in Harlow was that an interviewer was only able to carry out the interviews there towards the end of the fieldwork period and so had a relatively short time span available to call back on those away or out. Since other interviewers had achieved more than the target of twenty interviews, it was decided to close the fieldwork in order to keep to schedule on coding and tabulating.

Date preparation

Questionnaires were edited and coded by SCPR. In order to devise coding frames for the open-ended questions, listings of all the answers given in about fifty questionnaires were made. Draft coding frames were then designed by SCPR and discussed with the researcher.

When coding was complete, the data were transferred to eighty-column punched cards using three cards per respondent. The cards were then submitted to a computer edit procedure designed to check on the accuracy of the coding, consistency of responses and correct filtering procedures.

The Analysis

The analysis specification was designed by Clare Ungerson. Because of the small sample size, only certain questions were tabulated by breakdown groups.

Some of the breakdown groups were designed in several ways in order to provide data comparable with those supplied by the Stress Area Survey and with published statistics.

The following definition of household type was used for both the Stress Area and Migrants' Surveys.

Household Type as defined for the Stress Area Survey

(a) Persons living alone under 65
(b) Persons living alone over 65
(c) Married couples living alone in which head of household under 45
(d) Married couples living alone in which head of household 45–64
(e) Married couples living alone in which head of household 65+
(f) Households consisting of adults related to head of household but excluding children of head of household

(g) Parent(s) with unmarried children, eldest child under 16
(h) Parent(s) with married children or youngest child over 15
(i) Non-family groups
(j) Miscellaneous

The Cullingworth definitions[1] were also used for the Migrant's Survey but were not analysed in this book.

[1] J. B. Cullingworth, *English Housing Trends* (Bell, 1965)

INDEX

Index

The expressions in this index of 'New Towns' and 'Expanding Towns' are treated synonymously under New Towns. The letter-by-letter system has been adopted.